APOSTOLIC
EQUIPPING
DIMENSION

Equipping And Deploying Every Believer

by

JONAS CLARK

A SPIRIT OF LIFE CLASSIC

APOSTOLIC EQUIPPING DIMENSION

Equipping And Deploying Every Believer
ISBN 1-886885-08-7

Copyright © 2001 by Jonas Clark

Published by Spirit of Life Publishing
27 West Hallandale Beach Blvd.
Hallandale, Florida
33009-5437, U.S.A.
(954) 456-4420

01 02 03 04 05 06 07 ♦ 07 06 05 04 03 02 01

ABOUT
THE AUTHOR

The anointing on his life is both bold and strong. Jonas' great passion is to take this gospel of the kingdom into all the world. Fortitude and God's grace have taken the ministry international, carrying a message of divine impact and reform for this generation into over twenty-three nations. Jonas is...

pioneer of the Global Cause Network (GNC), a fellowship of over 58 churches around the world of like precious faith.

senior editor of The Ambassador Journal (www.catchlife.org), the New Apostolic Voice for the 21st Century. An internet magazine and prophetic journal sent to thousands of leaders in more than 62 countries.

a prolific writer who has authored many books with an apostolic and prophetic voice that are catching the attention of the church.

founder of Spirit of Life Publishing which provides critical learning resources, educational and informational materials throughout the nations.

pioneer of The Harvest Strategy, a reforming ministry structure for city-wide evangelism.

founder of Spirit of Life Ministries in Hallandale Beach, Florida an apostolic training center.

As a revivalist, his desire is to see the nations of the world impacted and changed by the power of God. Jonas has been in the ministry for seventeen years. He is blessed with his beautiful wife Rhonda and three daughters Natasha, Nichole and Natalie.

THIS BOOK
IS DEDICATED TO

The invading and occupying
teams of Spirit of Life Ministries.
You are awesome!

"And he gave some, apostles; and some, prophets; and some, evangelists; and some, pastors and teachers; {12} For the perfecting of the saints, for the work of the ministry, for the edifying of the body of Christ" (Ephesians 4:11-12 KJV).

CONTENTS

The Spirit of God through the apostolic dimension is transforming our motivations, orientations and specifically the way we look at the local church and our ministries.

With the rise of bishops came the theft of the believers' rights to follow the leading of the Holy Spirit in regards to ministry.

The gathered believers in a local apostolic center are the epic center of repentance, fervent prayer, prophetic decrees, apostolic establishment, spiritual warfare, revelation, praise, worship and spirit life.

Somehow we got 'deploy into the city' confused with 'gather to a building.' We confused 'equipped to do' with 'to have knowledge of without action' and 'go out' with 'hide out.'

Not only does the Holy Spirit assign metrons (ministry assignments) in specific territories for churches and believers (sent ones) to occupy, he also gives ample grace to back up those assignments.

Apostolic believers have a visible faith. They know how to take action and move beyond well wishing prayers and take hold of the situation at hand. They are solution minded and results-oriented.

Once we understand that Jesus backs us up when we speak and act on his word then we can live a victorious Christian life. We can demonstrate that we are believers with authority.

Evangelism is telling someone the good news that Jesus Christ died for our sins, was raised from the dead and is now extending forgiveness of sins to all who would believe.

There is a time to pray quietly and privately, but there is also a time to pray fervently and corporately. The apostolic equipping dimension will release a spirit of prayer into your life.

God is giving us effective strategies tailored for specific regions, territories and nations. He is the God of strategies and we can expect him to teach us how to succeed.

More than any other structure, apostolic teams and small groups give every person a way to minister their gifts. Apostolic teams take the church out of the building and into the city.

Jesus is our pattern for the greatest of all apostolic leaders. He took twelve ordinary men with various personalities, weaknesses, flaws and strengths and transformed them into a dynamic, world-changing revolutionary team.

What makes apostolic worship so different is not necessarily the music itself but rather the spiritual realm that it takes you into. That realm has more 'punch in the praise' and more 'depth in the worship.'

INTRODUCTION

Once it was rare to find anything written about the ministry of the apostle. The teaching of most denominations was even to deny their existence. When there was any teaching it was limited to the recognition of the 12 apostles of the Lamb and of the Apostle Paul who was chosen by the Holy Spirit to replace the traitor, Judas.

Today there are many books being written on the subject of modern day apostles. One of the most puzzling things to me is the lack of literature on the apostle's function that impacts ministry structure. It's nice to know that there are apostles, but what happens after they show up? What should we as believers expect to see? In this study I want to capture the apostolic equipping dimension. If an apostle is a reformer then it is safe to assume that he would also be an instrument of change. This environment of change *is* the apostolic dimension.

But what then would be that change? Could we expect a change in our orientation of ministry and how every believer fits into it? To focus on information about an apostle and not embrace the ministry of an apostle is vanity. In this book we will explore some of the changes that are being introduced by that apostolic spirit. We will

1

also discover the epic struggle of the apostle's calling to give the ministry back to the ordinary believers.

So we will discover that as we enter the apostolic equipping dimension our perception of ministry changes. The word informs us that the times just before the return of the Lord will be filled with reformation and restoration. Therefore we can expect Jesus' church to be set in order and brought back to its normal condition.

This book is about the equipping of every believer to do the work of ministry and to bring the ordinary Christian back to an understanding of his position of authority as a believer. It is also to explore the depths of an effective fervent prayer life and to reveal that our God is the God of effective strategies.

Jesus is building stronghold churches that are filled with strong, empowered and deployed believers. These believers are actively being prepared to be sent to reap the end time harvest. So in the following pages, let's enter the apostolic equipping dimension.

From South Florida,

Jonas Clark

CHAPTER 1

APOSTOLIC RESTORATION

The Spirit of God through the apostolic dimension is transforming our motivations, orientations, and specifically the way we look at the local church and our ministries.

Some have said that the greatest changes in history regarding the way we have church are taking place right now. I agree. Yet seldom does anyone give a clear description of what those changes are. If we are in a time of apostolic change and restoration, then what can we expect to see changed and restored?

I am convinced that God is restoring the apostle's ministry to the church but in order to understand apostles we need to take a strong look at their function and the impact that their ministry will have on the church.

It is difficult to separate the title from the function. In the days ahead many will take on apostolic titles but it will be the function that will separate, define and confirm the

3

ministry of an apostle. So with this in mind, let's explore the exciting world of the apostolic equipping dimension.

APOSTOLIC LEADERS ENTER UNCHARTED TERRITORIES OF RISK

We have heard a lot about the times of restoration. The scripture declares, "Whom the heaven must receive until the times of restoration of all things, which God hath spoken by the mouth of all his holy prophets since the world began" (Acts 3:21 KJV). This scripture implies that there must be a restoration of things that will take place before Jesus' return.

> The word restoration simply means to straighten out thoroughly to a natural and normal condition.

So what exactly are some of the truths that are being restored today that are bringing us back to a normal condition? To begin with, there is...

♦a fresh focus on evangelism

♦discipleship (not just conver-
sions) as the goal of evangelism

♦the importance of a local
church where everyone is committed to being a builder rather
than a receiver of knowledge
only to advance one's personal
interest

♦the restoration of all five ascension gifts of apostles, prophets, evangelists, pastors and
teachers, working together to
advance the gospel

♦the restoration of apostolic
teams rather than the one-man-
only paradigm, lone ranger, or
individualist concept

♦an apostolic structure where
every willing and available believer can function and minister outside the four walls of the
local church

♦the royal priesthood of all believers

♦territories of spiritual jurisdiction

TRANSFORMATIONS

The Spirit of God through the apostolic dimension is transforming our motivations, orientations and specifically the way we look at the local church and our ministries. One's orientation speaks of a way of seeing. It deals with...

aspects

attitudes

bearings

exposures

points of view

postures

vision

To be oriented means...

placement

bearings

attitude

6

alignment

layout

position

arrangement

setup

For example, the orientation of the building is such that the windows face south. The orientation of the new employees is scheduled for next week. We were given orientation lectures.

With this new apostolic orientation that is being poured out by the Holy Spirit will come a different way of looking at our...

churches

ministries

territories

cities

callings

motives

It will also be a time of transition, adjustment, and reform. In this study we are going to learn in an apostolic context what Jesus meant when he said, "Go ye into all the world" (Mark 16:15). I wonder how many people actually believe that this is a personal word for their life. Is it a commandment or simply a divine suggestion to those who might be able to find a few minutes of spare time? Or is it a command only to a select few who are specialists in some ministry? Some professional? The clergy? I personally believe that evangelism (*go ye*) should be the primary focus of our lives, local churches and ministries.

> The fruit of a passionate love and relationship with Jesus will always be demonstrated by a heart to spread the good news.

Yes, the church is a place of refuge, refreshing, and celebration, but it is also a place of leadership training, discipling, spiritual equipping, and deploying of every believer.

> The local church is an apostolic center. A center is the point around which everything revolves.

8

Moreover, evangelism is *not* having another conference that blesses only those who are already born again. I am not saying that we should not bless and strengthen the body of Christ, but I am saying that many meetings and ministry activities are being held that simply never reach the lost or the unchurched.

APOSTLES ARE AGENTS OF CHANGE

It is evident that we are continuing to shuffle the same group of believers from one conference to the next. It looks good because there are many people involved, but is it effective? Some important questions to ask are:

Is our orientation of ministry correct?

What pattern of ministry are we perpetuating?

Could we be deceived into thinking that every conference and seminar is equipping the people for the work of ministry? What paradigm (model or pattern) of ministry are we promoting?

Do we need to do something different?

COMPELLING ANTAGONIST

Jesus said, "...go out into the highways and hedges, and compel them to come in, that my house may be filled" (Luke 14:23 KJV). The Greek word for compel is *anagkazo* meaning to...

be forceful

threaten

entreat

drive

compel

From the word *anagkazo* we get the English word antagonist. In a positive sense an antagonist is one who is persistent and never gives up. As you can see from this scripture the spirit of evangelism is an action word (*anagkazo*) meaning to use whatever means necessary to reach the city and fill God's house. So are you a compelling

10

antagonist when it comes to reaching your city with the gospel? Have you taken hold of your responsibility as a believer to be a builder of God's house? Do you recognize that the advancement of the gospel will not happen without your cooperation? Or does that work belong to someone else? The Bible speaks of a time of the restoration of all things.

All of this leads us into the next chapter to explore the very thing that is currently being challenged and brought back into its proper order by the apostolic spirit, the bishop paradigm.

CHAPTER 2

THE REFORMATION CONTINUES

With the rise of bishops came the theft of the believers' rights to follow the leading of the Holy Spirit in regards to ministry.

American denominational churches have lost over one-forth of all their members.[1] Many pastors stand gazing at large segments of their congregations who stare back at them each Sunday morning as being spectators only. Many are loving and faithful to God yet there still remains an incredible challenge to move them out of a spectator only mentality into an anoint me, send me apostolic mindset. So what is the problem? Why is it that so many good people are content to sit idly by and watch? The answer is...

the priesthood of all believers has been relinquished to professionals (the clergy).

But how did this happen? Where did this

clergy structure of ministry come from? Why do we have church the way we have it today? Let's take a look back into our history to discover some powerful truths.

The main stronghold in Western churches is the loss of the truth of the priesthood of every believer. The word declares...

> "But ye are a chosen generation, a royal priesthood, an holy nation, a peculiar people; that ye should show forth the praises of him who hath called you out of darkness into his marvelous light:" (1 Peter 2:9 KJV)

A PARTIAL REFORMATION

Many understand the Reformation of Martin Luther, John Calvin, Ulrich Zwingli, and many others of the 16th Century whose motto was...

Sola gratia, by grace alone

Sola fide, through faith alone

Sola Scriptura, according to scripture alone

Soli Deo Gloria, for God's Glory alone [2]

During this period, approximately 400 years ago, the church underwent a partial reformation as men of God attempted to return Christianity to the authority of Scripture. Their struggle was...

> to prove the Holy Bible as the inerrant and infallible rule of faith and practice for the Christian

> to break people free from the assumption that ordinary Christians were not good enough to approach God

> to abolish the teaching that salvation was mediated *and* maintained through a priest via sacraments [3]

In effect, to place all of Christianity under the authority of God's word.

APOSTOLIC SUCCESSION

Yet few understand the titanic battle the reformers faced in opposing the false teaching of apostolic succession in their day. This paradigm had existed for hundreds of years. Sometime around Constantine's placement as emperor in 306 AD and the Coun-

15

cil of Nicene in 325 AD, the priesthood of all believers was usurped by the institution of a series of bishops. These bishops were thought to be direct descendants of the apostles through ordination conducted by the laying on of hands. It was said of these bishops that they were...

> "by divine right, an order superior to, distinct from, and having powers, authority and rights incompatible with presbyters (pastors)." [4]

> "(Bishops were) the sole successors of the apostles as ordainers of other ministers and governors both of pastors and people." [5]

With the rise of these bishops came the theft of the believer's rights to follow the leading of the Holy Spirit in regards to ministry. One counter reformationist stated,

> "It is not lawful without the bishop, neither to baptize, nor to celebrate the holy communion. He that does *anything* without his knowledge, ministers unto the devil" Ignatius (Italics added).[6]

These bishops were the new popes of territories and with their rise came...

a disappearing of the priesthood of all believers

a separation of responsibilities and duties

a different orientation towards ministry

new words like clergy and laity

a religious structure of ministry

control and religious tyranny

One can only imagine the opportunity for corruption since salvation was mediated by a priest. There were those ordained and anointed to do and those called only to listen and to watch. Herein lies the mystery of a spectator-only, bless-me-only, one-man-only paradigm of Christianity.

So we ascertain that the 16th Century brought a partial reformation. However, the breaking free of the one-man-only structure of controlling bishops was never accomplished. Why? The reformers had their hands full. Because of the false teaching on

17

apostolic succession, it appears the reformers threw out the baby with the bath water and declared the end of the ministry of the apostle altogether. By the 18th Century it was standard practice to hear statements such as...

> "the office of the apostles perished with the apostles."
> Pastor Henry Dodwell 18th Century Wesleyan Minister

With the reformers' failure to bring about an understanding of the necessity for a structural change of ministry within the local church, they were never able to return the ministry to the believer. So in effect there was a strengthening of the one-man-only structure of ministry.

The influence of this bishop paradigm still exists today in our contemporary Protestant churches. Examples would be...

> we bring our lost loved ones to the pastor/priest for him to lead them to Jesus.

> when someone is sick we don't pray for them ourselves instead we deliver the prayer request to the pastor/priest.

we think that church attendance is the end of our service
to God and that evangelism or
ministry should be left to the
clergy.

we hire pastors/priests to visit
the sick, care for the widows and
orphans, etc.

we have been reduced to spectators only.

The traditional thinking of a typical Protestant church member is that the church is
owned by the people (not Rome) who in turn
hire a pastor/priest to do their ministry for
them. Of course since they are Protestant
and not Catholics they, the church board
and congregation, would maintain an ongoing evaluation of the pastor's activities
subject to *their* continued approval.

So we discover that for 1700 years the
church has perpetuated a structure which
is not designed to include the believers in
the work of the ministry.

Again, the paradigm is one which draws
people to a building to watch — thus the
spectator only mindset. Therefore the existing structure of the church is not an apostolic design of equipping and sending, but
of drawing to watch.

We have had two thousand years to reach this world with the gospel and have yet to succeed. Why? Because it requires all of us to be involved. In order to reach this world with the gospel, there must be a restoration of the priesthood of all believers. This is the natural order that the Holy Spirit is restoring. So in short, what is the royal priesthood of all believers? It is that...

man can approach God directly and has no need of a mediating priest other than Jesus Christ. [7]

every born again believer is called into ministry. [8]

we are to speak to each other about God while calling each other to repentance and faith.

we are earthly representatives of God and called to intercede before God for one another. [9]

we are all ambassadors of Jesus Christ. [10]

we are all our brother's keeper.

Yes, our orientation is changing. We are entering a new apostolic reformation. This reformation will introduce a framework that will enable *every* believer to become involved in ministry. It will usher in the restoration of the priesthood of all believers.

> WE HAVE HAD TWO THOUSAND YEARS TO REACH THIS WORLD WITH THE GOSPEL AND HAVE YET TO SUCCEED. WHY?

Remember, the doctrine of the priesthood of the believer in no way contradicts the biblical understanding of the role, responsibility, and authority of the church's "set man" which is seen in the command of the local church in Hebrews 13:17, "Obey your leaders, and submit to them; for they keep watch over your souls, as those who will give an account."

In the next chapter we will take a look at the governing dynamic of local apostolic churches.

Notes

1 Roberta Hestenes, President Eastern College, St. Davids, Pennsylvania

2 See appendix A for scriptural references

3 Roman Catholics teach seven channels of God's grace called sacraments that are necessary for salvation. They are baptism, Eucharist, penance, holy orders, holy matrimony, confirmation, and anointing for the sick .

4 Thomas Powell on *Apostolic Succession* 1845

5 Ibid.

6 Ibid.

7 Hebrews 4:14-16

8 2 Timothy 4:2

9 James 5:16

10 2 Corinthians 5:20

CHAPTER 3

THE GOVERNING DYNAMIC

The gathered believers in a local apostolic center are the epic center of repentance, fervent prayer, prophetic decrees, apostolic establishment, spiritual warfare, revelation, praise, worship and spirit life.

This brings us into the governing aspect of the local apostolic church. *All of God's people are ministers!* Many people don't understand the apostolic governing dynamic of a local church. Many believers have isolated themselves and seldom think about reaching beyond their own immediate families and into the harvest fields around them. Mostly church has been reduced to a Sunday morning only routine. Many attend church only to hide from the cares of this world. Others because it seems to be the right thing to do. Others only to receive something. Therefore church attendance becomes a spectator, consumer, bless-me-only event void of builders. With this religious mindset one church seems to be as

23

good as another. However this is not the case in apostolic churches who understand their unique purpose. To them it is not about having church but being the church.

With the restoration of the apostolic dimension and the priesthood of every believer, it is clear that apostolic churches will raise up teams and small groups as an effective strategy to invade and occupy a city.

> Apostolic teams sent to invade.
> Small groups sent to build and
> to occupy.

To apostolically govern means...

> to rule by right of authority

> to exercise a directing or restraining influence

> to hold in check

> to regulate the speed of

> to exercise the function of government

So again we discover a different orientation of ministry within apostolic centers as we restore the priesthood of all believers. We are moving from passive spectators only to a place where we see ourselves as vital agents in the advancement of the gospel. *We are ascertaining that all believers are enabled to act.* We all have a ministry and a responsibility to advance the gospel and be builders of the local church.

CITY-WIDE EVANGELISM

To discover the depths of this one-man-only paradigm let's look at its influence on city wide evangelism efforts.

The evangelist comes into the city. All the cities's pastors assemble at the prayer breakfast listening to the evangelist speak of his vision to reach the lost in that city. The pastors return to their churches enlisting the support of their congregates to bring their lost loved ones and friends to the convention center for the evangelist to lead them to Christ. Hundreds are born again and everyone rejoices. The pastors return to their churches feeling as if they have been successful in reaching their city. At least they accomplished something.

Weeks later there can be heard questions in the church asking when the evangelist is returning back into town because another lost loved one needs to be led to Jesus.

Again, we have transferred the responsibility of the priesthood of all believers into the hands of a one-man-only paradigm. In

25

this case it is the gifted evangelist. Granted all efforts to bring someone to Jesus are important, but the responsibility of reaching the lost belongs to us all, not one person. I submit to the reader that this pattern of ministry is quickly becoming ineffective for reaching the lost and building churches.

AS IT GOES WITH THE LOCAL CHURCH, SO GOES IT WITH THE CITY

Research has shown that, across the board, the number of those who make first-time decisions for Christ at a city-wide evangelistic campaign and who subsequently become responsible members of local churches, runs between 3 percent and 16 percent.[1] Less than 1 percent of the "born again" believers in America have accepted Jesus Christ as a result of watching evangelistic television.[2] I am not against Christian television or city-wide evangelistic campaigns. I am simply making a point. One minister told me that he has conducted a million surveys asking the question, "How did you come to Christ?" Overwhelmingly 95 percent state that they came to Jesus through the personal witness of a friend or relative![3] This is 'case in point' for the importance of the restoration of the priesthood of all believers who are sent out (*apo-stello*) into the harvest fields from a strong local apostolic governing church. It has been well said, "As it goes with the local church, so goes it with the city."

Yes, as the priesthood of all believers is being restored to its natural order in the church, our orientation of ministry is being challenged. But with this challenge shall come new refreshing strategies for reaching the lost, discipleship methods, leadership development, and the building of apostolic centers.

STRONGHOLD CHURCHES

> "And I say also unto thee, That thou art Peter, and upon this rock I will build my church; and the gates of hell shall not prevail against it" (Matthew 16:18 KJV).

Jesus prophesied that he was going to build His church and that the gates of hell would not prevail. There is a church that Jesus is building. His church is a stronghold of righteousness. A lighthouse of His presence. A beacon of hope to a lost world with an apostolic equipping dimension.

Oftentimes we hear of places in our cities that are demonic strongholds. Many

27

avoid even entering these areas because of the potential danger of being harmed. We might label an area prevalent with drugs, prostitution, decadence, violence, poverty, and gangs as being demonic strongholds. I contend that Jesus is also building strongholds. His are righteous strongholds, apostolic centers that can be seen in every city and territory throughout the world. A stronghold is...

> a fortified place (Proverbs 18:10)

> a place with a concentration of spiritual warriors (1 Chronicles 12)

> a house of prayer and intimacy with our Lord (Isaiah 56:7)

> a gathering place of sent ones (Luke 10:2)

Sadly, some do not understand the purpose of the local church. Some see the local church as being owned by the people who then hire a pastor/priest to minister to them. It is a place of arts and crafts, Christmas decorations, music specials, chicken dinners, and home coming celebrations. Where the supernatural apostolic dimension has been replaced by...

dead religious programs

lifeless traditions

vain opinions of men

But now the Spirit of God is changing our orientation so that we recognize the local church as God's...

place of gathered authority

It is the home base for every ministry. Jesus has given every believer authority. We are that gathering of believers because we are doing what it takes to make a difference in our cities. The church is not a building. The devil has spent years usurping the believer's authority with religious form that has been centered around a one-man-only pattern of ministry. The word of God teaches us to guard ourselves from a form of godliness.

"Having a form of godliness, but denying the power thereof: from such turn away" (2 Timothy 3:5 KJV).

Jesus is building his victorious church. The word declares, "That he might present it to himself a glorious church, not having

29

spot, or wrinkle, or any such thing; but that it should be holy and without blemish" (Ephesians 5:27 KJV).

The gathered believers in a local apostolic center are the epic center of repentance, fervent prayer, prophetic decrees, apostolic establishment, spiritual warfare, revelation, praise, worship, and spirit life. Like a furnace in a steam-powered locomotive, gathered on-fire believers of the local church fuel the mighty power of effective apostolic ministry. Without the believers working together with the Holy Spirit there is no movement. They are, "the wheel within the wheel" (Ezekiel 1:16).

It is everyone's duty to be planted in a strong local church and take responsibility for its success. Gathered together with a common cause, these represent and demonstrate God's wisdom and purpose. Scripture declares, "now unto the principalities and powers in heavenly places might be *known by the church* the manifold wisdom of God" (Ephesians 3:10 KJV Italics added).

In the ensuing chapter we will explore the very important ministry of the priesthood of all believers.

GOD GIVES EVERY
BELIEVER SPIRITUAL AUTHORITY

Notes

[1] C. Peter Wagner, "Apostles of the City," (Colorado Springs CO. Wagner Publications, 2000), P.31.

[2] George Barna, "Marketing the Church," (Colorado Springs, CO. Navpress, 1988),P.53.

[3] Bob Weiner of Weiner Ministries International

CHAPTER 4

PRIESTHOOD OF ALL BELIEVERS

*Somehow we got 'deploy into the city' con-
fused with 'gather to a building.' We confused
'equipped to do' with 'to have knowledge of
without action' and 'go out' with 'hide out.'*

For years now, success in ministry often has been determined by one's ability to draw people to a building. With this concept of ministry millions of dollars are spent looking for and promoting the best draw in town. By focusing on drawing only we have lost our ability to mobilize and deploy the believers into the work of ministry, because unknowingly we have presented a bless-me-only structure to the people. The only thing people think they are called to do is show up to the building and watch.

In other words, we prepare the church where the only necessary requirement of the people is to assemble in a beautiful building, pay one's tithes, quietly pray and listen to the preacher minister a ten minute moti-

vational message; then we go home and repeat the same cycle for forty more years.
Boring!

Please understand, I am certainly not
against assembling ourselves together, praying and tithing. These things should go
without saying. Of course it is important to
hear the word of the God, but there is even
more. There is an apostolic equipping dimension to ministry. There is a deployment
of the believers. There is the mobilization of
the troops. There is the raising up of the
sons of God.

Moreover, we need to listen to the demand
of the Holy Spirit to grow up spiritually. The
scripture is very clear. It is our duty to equip
every believer for the work of the ministry.
To deploy *every* believer into the priesthood.

> "And he gave some, apostles;
> and some, prophets; and some,
> evangelists; and some, pastors
> and teachers; {12} For the per-
> fecting of the saints, for the work
> of the ministry, for the edifying
> of the body of Christ:"
> (Ephesians 4:11-12 KJV)

EQUIP AND DEPLOY

Ministers of the gospel are God's gifts to
the church. They are not to dominate the

people of God (1 Peter 5:3) but are set in the church to equip them *and* deploy them into active works of service and ministry (Ephesians 4:11, 12).

**IT IS OUR DUTY
TO EQUIP EVERY BELIEVER
FOR THE WORK OF THE MINISTRY**

Somehow we got 'deploy into the city' confused with 'gather to a building.' We confused 'equipped to do' with 'to have knowledge of without action' and 'go out' with 'hide out.' Then we transferred our responsibility 'to work' in the ministry and replaced it with 'hire someone' to do it for us. *Success in ministry in the 21st Century will no longer be determined by how many are sitting in a building, but by how many have been sent.*

All believers are a holy priesthood called by God to offer up spiritual sacrifices as priests (1 Peter 2:5). All believers are in essence a royal priesthood (1 Peter 2:9) and the sons of God (1 Peter 1:3, 23; Galations 3:26) through faith in Christ Jesus. They are all priests and kings (1 Peter 2:9). All born again believers have received the call as ambassadors of Christ (2 Corinthians 5:20).

An ambassador is the highest ranking diplomatic representative appointed by a country or government.

Every born again believer is qualified to be spiritually equipped and deployed for works of service. The word, in speaking about all believers declares, "we have different gifts, according to the grace given us. If a man's gift is prophesying, let him use it in proportion to his faith" (Romans 12:6 KJV).

Every believer has been given something that will help advance the gospel.

"But the manifestation of the Spirit is given to *every man* to profit withal" (1 Corinthians 12:7 Italics added).

"But unto *every one* of us is given grace according to the measure of the gift of Christ" (Ephesians 4:7 Italics added).

"As *every man* hath received the gift, even so minister the same one to another, as good stewards of the manifold grace of God" (1 Peter 4:10 KJV Italics added).

The doctrine of the priesthood of the believer does not usurp the responsibility of an apostolic set man in the local church. The set man (Numbers 27:16) of the local church is called of God to lead that local church. "Take heed therefore unto yourselves, and to all the flock, over the which the Holy Ghost hath made you overseers, to feed the church of God, which he hath purchased with his own blood" (Acts 20:28 KJV).

> The restoration of the church as a royal priesthood of all believers will never be completed as long as the saints come not to minister, but to be ministered to only.

Nor will it be completed with a believer's mindset that thinks that it is more convenient to hire someone to visit the sick, comfort the afflicted, restore the erring, care for the widows and orphans, proclaim the glad tidings, and minister unto the believers; than it is to do these things personally. The royal priesthood (all believers) must be made to realize that...

> their rights as sons must never be surrendered to another

the task of bringing the world to Jesus belongs to every believer

to be born again means to be in the ministry

In the next chapter we will study the local churches assigned places of spiritual jurisdiction known as *metrons*.

CHAPTER 5

METRONS

Not only does the Holy Spirit assign metrons (ministry assignments) in specific territories for churches and believers (sent ones) to occupy, he also gives ample grace to back up those assignments.

It is interesting to think that God actually assigns local churches places of spiritual jurisdiction and influence. Apostolic churches are not just in the city by chance. They have been *set* there by the wisdom of God. When we begin to understand our responsibility of reaching the territory of our ministries then we can take on a different orientation to ministry, and more fully discern the overall scope of the local church.

God does give authority and grace to occupy our territories. How we look at our cities is critical in this hour. Apostolic churches are given assigned places of spiritual jurisdiction known as *metrons*. The understanding of metrons is important for every believer to grasp because it is the believers themselves who are sent (*apo-stello*) to occupy these territories. The apostolic dimension of a local governing church activates and empowers every believer as sent ones to invade and occupy these metrons. Let's examine an important scripture and some key Greek words to study this out.

> "For we dare not make ourselves of the number, or compare ourselves with some that commend themselves: but they measuring (judging) themselves by themselves, and comparing themselves among themselves, are not wise. {13} But we will not boast of things without our measure, but according to the **measure** *(metron)* of the rule *(kanon)* which God hath distributed to us, a **measure** *(metron)* to reach even unto you (2 Corinthians 10:12-13 KJV).

This is a very revealing scripture. The Greek word *metron* means...

a portioned off measure

a determined extent

a measure or limit

The Greek word *kanon* as seen above means...

> a rule or line

> a fixed space within limits

> where one's power of influence is confined

> an assigned province

> one's sphere of activity

So we learn:

A *metron* is clearly defined as a measured out boundary. It can be likened to a fenced in area of authority or an assigned territory.

This same area would also be known as a place of spiritual jurisdiction and influence assigned to a local church, person, ministry, apostolic team, etc., by the Holy Spirit. Therefore a *metron* is...

> ♦ a target area

> ♦ a place where one has an assigned scope of ministry and spiritual influence

> ♦ a marked off territory

41

♦ a place of focused spiritual and natural activity

♦ a place with marked off boundaries

♦ a territory with specific limits of assignment and responsibilities that are known as *kanons*

♦ a place of spiritual jurisdiction

Simply stated, a metron is your place of ministry assignment.

GRACE FOR MINISTRY

Not only does the Holy Spirit assign *metrons* (ministry assignments) in specific territories for churches and believers (sent ones) to occupy, he also gives ample grace to back up those assignments.

"But unto every one of us is given grace according to the measure *(metron)* of the gift of Christ" (Ephesians 4:7 KJV).

This is a very important verse. Here we learn that God gives us grace amply sufficient for the territory or place of our assignment.

42

So we learn that:

> Grace, favor and everything we
> need to be successful in minis-
> try is given to us to accomplish
> our task when we are within our
> metrons.

When things are hard in ministry remember that when God assigns a ministry task or a ministry territory he surely provides everything necessary to be successful in accomplishing your mission in your assigned metron.

Therefore, grace is given according to the metron you're assigned to. The harder the territory, the more grace given. It doesn't make any difference how hard the area is or the task at hand. You will find grace sufficient when you draw near to God. Much difficulty, much grace. Much hardship, much grace. Much sin, much grace.

> Grace is the power to advance
> beyond our own abilities.

So how do we obtain this grace? Through faith and prayer. The scripture declares, "Let us therefore come boldly unto the throne of grace, that we may obtain mercy, and find grace to help in time of need" (Hebrews 4:16 KJV).

APOSTOLIC PARADIGM

As 21st Century apostolic churches emerge there will be at least four specific paradigm changes taking place within the local church.

1. Perhaps one of the most profound will be a breaking free from the one-man-only paradigm. This paradigm requires all of the church's marketing efforts and resources to be used in drawing people to a building to be taught by one gift.

2. The second will powerfully effect the goal of evangelism and take it from just getting a decision for Christ into raising a disciple of Christ.

3. There will be a major shift in the church from an inward focus to an outward focus of ministry. Not only will the church be a place where people can gather together to worship and be refreshed but it will also be the place where apostolic strategies and goals are set, as believers are activated and released into ministry.

4. Various apostolic teams will be built, activated and sent out into the surrounding city and into the nations of the world.

Lyle Schaller, church growth visionary, says, "The old pattern of individuals working alone in their own isolated empires is being replaced by teams."[1]

Apostle John Eckhardt commenting on the rise of teams says, "There are apostolic teams, prophetic teams, evangelistic teams, deliverance teams, prayer teams, praise and worship teams, teaching teams, and pastoral teams." [2]

GRACE IS THE POWER TO ADVANCE BEYOND YOUR OWN ABILITIES

A true apostolic paradigm is one that...

gathers

teaches

equips

assigns

targets

builds

shapes

deploys teams

disciples

THE APOSTOLIC EQUIPPING DIMENSION

Today thousands of churches have no apostolic structure in place to move people beyond a teaching or pastoring only structure, into one that sends the believers into the harvest fields. But this is changing now in the 21st Century's apostolic reformation. The emerging apostolic leaders are embracing these mighty truths as they get ready to fulfill the Great Commission.

Just as John the Baptist declared in his generation that the ax was being laid to the root, so it is in our generation.

> "And now also the ax is laid unto the root of the trees: therefore every tree which bringeth not forth good fruit is hewn down, and cast into the fire" (Matthew 3:10 KJV).

Now let's take a look at the spirit of an apostolic believer.

Notes
[1] Reggie McNeal, "Revolution in Leadership," (Nashville, TN. Abingdon Press, 1998), P12.
[2] Ibid, P34.

CHAPTER 6

APOSTOLIC BELIEVERS

Apostolic believers have a visible faith. They know how to take action and move beyond well wishing prayers and take hold of the situation at hand. They are solution minded and results oriented.

It is not enough to discuss the restoration of the priesthood of all believers without capturing the apostolic spirit of the end time priesthood. Apostolic believers are different. Like Joshua and Caleb they possess a different spirit and have a different orientation. In a positive sense they are radicals, extremist and nonconformist when it comes to obstacles that buffet the advancement of the gospel.

> "But my servant Caleb, because he had another spirit with him, and hath followed me fully, him will I bring into the land whereinto he went; and his seed

shall possess it" (Numbers 14:24 KJV).

I have noticed that there are three words that many have dropped from their vocabulary because of religious perception and opinions. Yet these three words help capture and express the apostolic dimension. They are...

radical

extremist

nonconformist

Let's take a look at each of these three words.

RADICAL

When we hear the word radical we immediately think of someone who acts crazy, is unstable, or has just lost their mind completely. But that is a definition formed by negative religious perceptions and opinions. Being radical simply means that you...

desire extreme change in your current situation.

If you are sick and desire to be completely well then you are looking for extreme change. That is radical thinking and there is nothing wrong with it. If you are thousands of dollars in debt and you desire to have all of your bills paid, then you are looking for a radical change in your financial circumstances. That too is fine.

> Apostolic believers are radical thinkers who demonstrate radical actions.

The Bible shows us some radical actions that got the attention of our Lord Jesus Christ. Let's take a look at the radical actions of an apostolic team, the friends of a man with a crippling palsy (Mark 2). When the friends of the crippled man could not get their friend to Jesus through the front door of the house, they climbed up on the roof and broke it to pieces so that they could lower him to Jesus.

Apostolic believers are not afraid of doing things that have never been done. They find solutions to problems. That was a radical action by these radical believers. I am sure that the crowd that was gathered inside that house as furious with them. Yet Jesus honored this radical team's act of faith and demonstrated love by healing the man of palsy and forgiving his sin.

49

"When Jesus *saw their faith,* he said unto the sick of the palsy, son, thy sins be forgiven thee" (Mark 2:5 KJV Italics added).

Apostolic believers are true friends who take action. Their faith is visible. They move beyond well wishing prayers and take hold of the situation at hand. They are solution minded and results-oriented. Often accused of being unloving their love is demonstrated with a take charge perseverance. This apostolic team got the job done! They got their friend to Jesus.

EXTREMIST

Apostolic believers are extremist. They are completely sold out to God. What exactly is an extremist anyway? An extremist is one who will go to the cutting edge. This person is known as the ultimate pioneering adventurer.

An extremist is one who holds to a view that is far away from the main stream.

This doesn't mean that they are not sober minded and balanced. History is full of

Christians who would be labeled as extrem-
ists if they lived in our generation. They
were in fact God's revolutionary agents of
change.

Evan Roberts of the great Welsh
Revival saw himself as "the
Lord's special messenger who
would arouse the churches for
their task of saving the nation."

Charles Parham known as the
Father of Pentecost proclaimed,
"Speaking in tongues was the
evidence of the baptism of the
Holy Spirit."

John G. Lake missionary to Africa declared, "You can fill my
hand with them (germs) and I
will keep it under the micro-
scope, and instead of these
germs remaining alive, they will
die instantly."

Hudson Taylor in his quest to
reach Inland China started
wearing Chinese dress and even
shaved his head while keeping
only a pigtail that was weaved
into his own hair that he dyed
jet black.

Praying John Hyde missionary
to Northern India was often
times heard shouting, "Give me
souls, Oh God, or I die!"

Even today Reinhard Bonnke boldly declares, "All of Africa shall be saved!" His efforts to use the world's postal system to mail
the gospel to every home is definitely far from
the main stream of typical evangelism methods.

All of these people had extreme ideas outside of the main stream of Christian thinking in their generations, and the fear of not
being understood did not stop them. They
were apostolic believers who had entered an
apostolic dimension.

There are many today that God is raising up with extreme cutting edge ideas that
will bring about God's will for this generation.

I personally like the word extremist because the cutting edge of your walk with
God is the most exciting adventure that you
will ever have. One who is highly committed
and dedicated to the advancement of the
gospel of Jesus Christ would be considered
an extremist today by some. It has been said
that if you are not living on the cutting edge
then you are taking up too much room.

The Apostle Peter was an extremist. He saw Jesus and said, "Lord, if it be thou, bid me come unto thee on the water." That was an extreme request. Peter's orientation was different. This type of extreme request was as far away from the main stream of thinking as one could get. Who would ever consider asking Jesus such a thing?

EXTREME BELIEVERS
ASK GOD FOR EXTREME THINGS

Extreme believers ask God for extreme things. They are risk takers who enter realms of uncharted territories of faith. But at the response of Jesus to come, Peter boldly stepped out of the boat and walked on the water at the utter amazement of the other apostles (Matthew 14). What about you? Are you willing to step onto the cutting edge of your boat to see your needs met and to fulfill your destiny? Are you an apostolic believer? Jesus' commandment to come gave Peter his place of spiritual jurisdiction and grace to walk on his metron.

Sometimes when you write like this some take it as a license to be flaky and weird. That is not what this is all about. The point is that the apostolic equipping dimension will break you away from the main stream of dead traditional religious thinking and empower you to respond to Jesus in an extreme way to receive an extreme victory. Apostolic believers are risk takers. They walk on the water of their metrons.

NONCONFORMIST

The last word is nonconformist. Please don't confuse nonconformity with rebellion. Rebellion is a defiance or opposition to authority. A nonconformist is one who refuses to make himself similar to the main stream of public opinion. In short, a nonconformist does not blend. It is possible to be a nonconformist and not be in rebellion. Let's look at a nonconformist in the Word of God.

Blind Bartimaeus wanted to see again (Mark 10:46). He heard that Jesus was passing his way and cried out to him with a loud voice. "Jesus, thou son of David, have mercy on me!" The public was outraged. How dare this man shout out loud and disturb everyone else. "Shut up old man," was their cry. But Blind Bartimaeus cried out all the more. He refused to conform to the charges of the crowd around him. He needed his healing and he wasn't going to let the voices of the religious crowd stop him. He shouted all the more!

Blind Bartimaeus is a great example of a nonconformist. He needed his healing and

54

shouted a great deal more to get it. Was he bucking the religious crowd? Absolutely. But guess what? His willingness to buck the opposition stopped the master. Apostolic believers are perseverant. They don't let obstacles, difficulties, or discouragement stop them. They keep pressing in.

Bartimaeus was healed because he would not blend in. He was a nonconformist in the positive sense. When the religious spirit demanded his conformity, he resisted with such volume that it got Jesus' attention. Jesus approved of this nonconformist's faith and gave him eyesight (Mark 10).

Bartimaeus was a master overcomer (Revelations 12:11). To overcome means to win the struggle and carry off the victory. He made a decision and took action.

In summary, apostolic believers don't let lifeless religion rob them from receiving God's best. It is all right to be radical...

desiring extreme change from your current situation.

It is all right to be an extremist...

one who will go to the cutting edge of commitment and dedication to the advancement of the gospel of Jesus Christ.

It is OK to be a nonconformist...

refusing to conform yourself to
a dead religious image or public opinions of men.

In the next chapter we will study the
believer's authority.

CHAPTER 7

THE BELIEVER'S AUTHORITY

Once we understand that Jesus backs us up when we speak his word and act on his word then we can live a victorious Christian life. We can demonstrate that we are believers with authority.

Not only will the apostolic dimension bring a restoration of the priesthood of every believer (all Christians are ministers) it will also usher in an apostolic understanding and impartation of spiritual authority to every believer.

God gives every believer spiritual authority. If there is any subject that I have been personally persecuted for in my ministry it has to be in teaching that God gives every believer spiritual authority. There was a time in my life when I asked myself if I could do any thing to stop the circumstances that were raging against my life. I asked others questions, searched the word and prayed. Many people told me that suffering was the will of God, used to help teach me some kind of lesson. Others thought that whatever happened to me had to be the will of God. However I didn't believe it. I knew that God was a good God and the devil was a bad devil. Then one day I read this verse in the word of God.

> "Behold, I give unto you power *(exousia)* to tread on serpents and scorpions, and over all the power *(dunamis)* of the enemy: and nothing shall by any means hurt you" (Luke 10:19 KJV, Italics added).

You can see in the above verse that the word power is actually two different Greek words. One word for power is *exousia,* meaning authority. The other word for power is *dunamis,* meaning mighty power. Unfortunately the Bible translators did not help us understand this verse by translating both words as power.

Jesus is literally saying in this verse, "Behold, I give unto you *authority* to tread on serpents and scorpions, and over all the *power* of the enemy: and nothing shall by any means hurt you." So what is authority?

> Authority is the power or right to give a command!

Serpents and scorpions are symbols of evil spirits of wickedness and demonic powers. Jesus identifies them as our enemy. An enemy is one who hates you and desires to hurt you. The Apostle Paul teaches us, too that we have spiritual enemies that we wrestle against. Moreover when we wrestle against these demonic powers in the strength of the Lord we always win.

> "Finally, my brethren, be strong in the Lord, and in the power *(kratos)* of his might. {11} Put on the whole armor of God, that ye may be able to stand against the wiles of the devil. {12} For we wrestle not against flesh and blood, but against principalities, against powers *(exousia)*, against the rulers of the darkness of this world, against spiritual wickedness in high places. {13} Wherefore take unto you the whole armor of God, that ye may be able to withstand in the evil day, and having done all, to stand" (Ephesians 6:10-13 KJV).

Here again we see the use of two different words for power. *Kratos* in the above verse means strength. Paul is saying, "... be strong in the Lord and in the strength *(kratos)* of his might." Here we learn not to rely on our own natural strength but to draw on the spiritual strength that comes from the Lord.

AUTHORITY IS THE POWER OR RIGHT TO GIVE A COMMAND!

You cannot battle demonic powers in your flesh and win. Jesus is the power behind the written word. Once we understand that Jesus backs us up when we speak his word and act on his word then we can live a victorious Christian life. We can demonstrate that we are believers with authority.

Again, authority is the power or right to give a command. Don't spiritualize this. The ability to exercise your right to command *(exousia)* is activated when you understand that it is Christ who is living in you.

You are not alone! Jesus is not only in you but with you. If you are born again, you are not on your own. The Holy Spirit, that same spirit that raised Christ from the dead is living in you. If you don't understand your authority *(exousia)* as a believer, then the priesthood of all believers will mean little to you.

The Apostle Paul draws back the curtain of real life and teaches us what is happening behind the scenes in the spirit realm. However, as human beings walking on this earth we can exercise the authority given to us as we live out our daily lives. We do this by...

♦ soul winning

♦ believing God's word

♦ acting out what we believe

♦ doing the word

♦ speaking the word

♦ praying for ourselves and others

♦ binding and loosing through prayer

♦ casting out demons

♦ praying for the sick

Jesus has given us his mighty power. We are authorized *(exousia)* to use his word against all our enemies. We have the right to command and he will always back us up. Authority belongs to you. Jesus said, "Verily, verily, I say unto you, He that believeth on me, the works that I do shall he do also; and greater works than these shall he do; because I go unto my Father" (John 14:12 KJV).

The believer's authority is not just to give you some temporary relief. It is to launch you into an exciting active ministry. In the next chapter we will examine what it means to minister.

CHAPTER 8

HOW TO MINISTER

Evangelism is telling someone the good news that Jesus Christ died for our sins, was raised from the dead and is now extending forgiveness of sins to all who would believe.

The apostolic anointing will equip you to be a minister. Ministry is not just standing behind a pulpit on Sunday morning and preaching the gospel. Ministry has been glamorized and confined within the four walls of a local church, but ministry is really in the trenches, on the streets, out where the people live, at work and in the marketplace. You may never preach the gospel inside a church building but that does not mean that you are not called to play an active and vital role in ministry. Remember that you are being equipped for the work of ministry Ephesians 4:12. The Greek word for ministry is *diakonia* meaning to...

promote

proclaim

execute the will of another

It also means to meet the needs of others as a servant. But what exactly does it mean to minister? Let's examine just a few things that ministers do.

MINISTRY OF RECONCILIATION

Our first responsibility as ministers is to lead people to Jesus Christ and share our faith as ministers of reconciliation.

> "And all things are of God, who hath reconciled us to himself by Jesus Christ, and hath given to us the *ministry of reconciliation*; {19} To wit, that God was in Christ, reconciling the world unto himself, not imputing their trespasses unto them; and hath committed unto us the word of reconciliation" (2 Corinthians 5:18-19 KJV Italics added).

Reconciliation is the Greek word *katallage* meaning to restore the sinner back to favor with God. The word says that, "God so loved the world, that he gave his only begotten

Son, that whosoever believeth in him should not perish, but have everlasting life" (John 3:16 KJV). Who are those responsible to herald this good news of restoration? They are the ministers of God (all believers) who are active in promoting, proclaiming and executing his will.

> Evangelism is telling someone the good news that Jesus Christ died for our sins, was raised from the dead and is now extending forgiveness of sins to all who would believe.

The word says, "How then shall they call on him in whom they have not believed? and how shall they believe in him of whom they have not heard? and how shall they hear without a preacher? {15} And how shall they preach, except they be sent? as it is written, How beautiful are the feet of them that preach the gospel of peace, and bring glad tidings of good things!" (Romans 10:14-15 KJV).

All believers can preach (herald) the gospel, share the good news and bring glad tidings! Paul is teaching us that one cannot get to know Jesus unless someone shares the news. That someone is the ordinary believer.

As believers we represent a royal priesthood of ambassadors of Jesus. As we share our faith, the good news, the word of God and our personal testimonies, the Holy Spirit uses our testimony to penetrate even the hardest of hearts. As we share the truth of the gospel we either catch fish (souls) on the spot or plant seeds in people for a later harvest, but something always happens. Reaching the world with the gospel *is* the ministry.

INTERCESSION

Those who do the work of ministry intercede (pray) for others. To intercede is to plea or make a request on behalf of another. Ministers understand the power of intercession because it is part of the very nature of God.

> "And I sought for a man among them, that should make up the hedge, and stand in the gap before me for the land, that I should not destroy it: but I found none" (Ezekiel 22:30 KJV).

To intercede for another means to pray with the Holy Spirit to get prayer answers for others. The Apostle Paul said that he travailed in prayer again for the Galation believers.

> "My little children, of whom I
> travail in birth again until
> Christ be formed in you"
> (Galations 4:19 KJV).

From this verse we discover that Paul had such a heavy burden for the people in this church that he prayed that Christ (the anointed one) would be formed (*morphoo*) in them. Can you imagine the power of this intercession that so challenged these believers to be conformed into the image of Christ?

As Paul travailed it means that he felt the pains of child birth during this intense time of prayer. In fact his intercession was so powerful that, coupled with the Holy Spirit, it gave birth to new things, unlocked mysteries of God, destiny and purpose over the people. So we learn that ministers follow the leading of the Holy Spirit and intercede for others. "I exhort therefore, that, first of all, supplications, prayers, intercessions, and giving of thanks, be made for all men" (1 Timothy 2:1 KJV).

LAYING ON OF HANDS

Ministers follow the biblical pattern of laying hands on people. The laying on of hands is a scriptural pattern of impartation that is seen throughout the scriptures as a solid biblical doctrine.

"Of the doctrine of baptisms,
and of *laying on of hands*, and
of resurrection of the dead, and
of eternal judgment" (Hebrews
6:2 KJV Italics added).

Let's see some instances where ministers laid their hands on others in the scriptures. One of the last things that Jesus said
when speaking to believers was that they,
"shall lay hands on the sick and they shall
recover" (Mark 16:18). The pattern of the
laying on of hands as a ministry function is
also demonstrated in the lives of the
apostles.

"And *by the hands of the
apostles* were many signs and
wonders wrought among the
people" ("Acts 5:12 KJV Italics
added).

We see a transference of anointing when
Moses laid his hands on Joshua. The ministry of the laying on of hands was so important to God that he commanded Moses
to do it before all the congregation.

"And the LORD said unto
Moses, Take thee Joshua the
son of Nun, a man in whom is
the spirit, and lay thine hand

upon him... And he *laid his
hands upon him,* and gave him
a charge, as the LORD commanded by the hand of Moses"
(Numbers 27:18,23 KJV Italics
added).

When Barnabas and Paul were sent out
of the church in Antioch, the laying on of
hands released God's mighty power into this
apostolic team.

"As they ministered to the Lord,
and fasted, the Holy Ghost said,
Separate me Barnabas and
Saul for the work whereunto I
have called them. {3} And when
they had fasted and prayed, and
laid their hands on them, they
sent them away." (Acts 13:2-3
KJV Italics added)

When men were chosen as deacons in
the early church hands were laid on them
to set them apart for service.

"Whom they set before the
apostles: and when they had
prayed, they *laid their hands on
them*" (Acts 6:6 KJV Italics
added).

Jesus ministered to the sick by the laying on of his hands.

> "And when the sabbath day was come, he began to teach in the synagogue: and many hearing him were astonished, saying, From whence hath this man these things? and what wisdom is this which is given unto him, that even such mighty works are *wrought by his hands*? {3} Is not this the carpenter, the son of Mary, the brother of James, and Joses, and of Juda, and Simon? and are not his sisters here with us? And they were offended at him. {4} But Jesus said unto them, A prophet is not without honour, but in his own country, and among his own kin, and in his own house. {5} And he could there do no mighty work, save that he *laid his hands upon a few sick folk, and healed them*" (Mark 6:2-5 KJV Italics added).

It was well known throughout Jesus' ministry that there was always virtue (power) flowing through his hands. We can see this when one day Jesus was asked to place his hands on a deaf man.

> "And they brought unto him one that was deaf, and had an impediment in his speech; and they beseech him to *put his hand upon him*" (Mark 7:32 KJV Italics added).

Even the Apostle Paul experienced the personal ministry of having hands laid on him.

> "And Ananias went his way, and entered into the house; and *putting his hands on him* said, Brother Saul, the Lord, even Jesus, that appeared unto thee in the way as thou camest, hath sent me, that thou mightest receive thy sight, and be filled with the Holy Ghost" (Acts 9:17 KJV Italics added).

The laying on of hands is an important act of a minister. Never be afraid to do it because it is the Bible way to release God's mighty power. Signs and wonders are awaiting when you obey the scriptures to lay your hands on others.

PRAYER FOR THE SICK

Praying for those who are sick is an important aspect of a minister. It is God's desire to heal the sick and he will use you to pray for others who need healing. When teaching his disciples how to be ministers he said, "Heal the sick, cleanse the lepers, raise the dead, cast out devils: freely ye have received, freely give" (Matthew 10:8 KJV). Jesus is the same yesterday, today and forever (Hebrews 13:8). He is still healing the sick and requiring his ministers (those who execute his will) to take an active role.

> "And Jesus went about all Galilee, teaching in their synagogues, and preaching the gospel of the kingdom, and healing all manner of sickness and all manner of disease among the people" (Matthew 4:23 KJV).

> "That it might be fulfilled which was spoken by Esaias the prophet, saying, Himself took our infirmities, and bare our sicknesses" (Matthew 8:17 KJV).

> "Then Peter said, Silver and gold have I none; but such as I have give I thee: In the name of

Jesus Christ of Nazareth rise up and walk" (Acts 3:6 KJV).

"How God anointed Jesus of Nazareth with the Holy Ghost and with power: who went about doing good, and healing all that were oppressed of the devil; for God was with him" (Acts 10:38 KJV).

CASTING OUT DEMONS

Jesus gave every one of his ministers power to cast out demons. In today's society people are in desperate need of deliverance ministers. We must never forget that the *same* anointing that heals the sick, opens blind eyes and deaf ears, will also cast out demons.

Demons can never be talked out, negotiated out or manipulated out. You cannot make deals with them. They have a ministry of destruction and they must be cast out. The Greek word for cast out is *ekballo* meaning to...

violently drive out

expel by force

command to depart

73

The anointing to cast out demons has been given to all those who believe and walk in God's authority. The apostolic dimension will not tolerate nor ignore demonic spirits. All believers are authorized to use the name of Jesus and cast out devils.

Deliverance is one of the most neglected ministries in the church today. But it is one of the most important. Why? Because to really love people means that we want the very best for them. If there are demonic strongholds in the lives of people, there is no way to help the people get free outside of an effective deliverance ministry. Due to these demonic strongholds, many people continue to fall into the same old sins. In my book *COME OUT!*[1] I go into more detail in regards to deliverance. I wrote the book as a handbook for the serious deliverance minister.

> "And he said unto them, Go ye into all the world, and preach the gospel to every creature. {16} He that believeth and is baptized shall be saved; but he that believeth not shall be damned. {17} And these signs shall follow them that believe; In my name shall they *cast out devils*; they shall speak with new tongues; {18} They shall take up serpents; and if they drink any

deadly thing, it shall not hurt
them; they shall lay hands on
the sick, and they shall recover"
(Mark 16:15-18 KJV Italics
added).

REACHING THE WORLD WITH
THE GOSPEL IS THE MINISTRY!

"Behold, I give unto you power
to tread on serpents and scorpions, and over all the power of
the enemy: and nothing shall
by any means hurt you. {20}
Notwithstanding in this rejoice
not, that the spirits are subject
unto you; but rather rejoice,
because your names are written in heaven." (Luke 10:19-20
KJV)

From this verse we learn that evil spirits
are in fact subject unto every believer who
ministers the gospel. It is because your
name is written in the Lamb's book of life
that you have the authority to cast out demons. That's worth rejoicing about, too! Let's
help those we love by exercising our rights
to cast out demonic powers.

GET PEOPLE
FILLED WITH HOLY GHOST

> "But ye shall receive power
> (*dumanis*), after that the Holy
> Ghost is come upon you: and
> ye shall be *witnesses* unto me
> both in Jerusalem, and in all
> Judaea, and in Samaria, and
> unto the uttermost part of the
> earth." (Acts 1:8 KJV)

The Greek word for witness is *martus*.
This is where we get the English word martyr. A martyr is one willing to suffer and die
for their faith. This verse is teaching us that
after the Holy Ghost comes upon us that we
would receive such an infilling of the Holy
Spirit that we would be willing to even die
for the advancement of the cause of Christ.
This really captures the spirit in the scripture that declares, "And they overcame him
(Satan and demonic powers) by the blood of
the Lamb, and by the word of their testimony; and they loved not their lives unto
the death" Revelation 12:11 KJV).

Those who are born again may not be
filled with the Holy Spirit. We can see this
clearly as the Apostle Paul meets with believers who had never even heard about the
baptism of the Holy Ghost.

"He (Paul) said unto them, Have ye received the Holy Ghost *since ye believed?* And they said unto him, We have not so much as heard whether there be any Holy Ghost. {3} And he said unto them, Unto what then were ye baptized? And they said, Unto John's baptism. {4} Then said Paul, John verily baptized with the baptism of repentance, saying unto the people, that they should believe on him which should come after him, that is, on Christ Jesus. {5} When they heard this, they were baptized in the name of the Lord Jesus. {6} And when Paul had laid his hands upon them, the Holy Ghost came on them; and they spake with tongues, and prophesied" (Acts 19:2-6 KJV Italics added).

The Spirit of God will use you to lay your hands on people to be filled with the Holy Ghost, too. There are many other functions of a minister that you may want to study out such as...

♦pointing people to Jesus the author and finisher of their faith (Hebrews 12:2)

♦being a good listener

♦showing mercy and compassion (1 Peter 3:8)

♦visiting and calling those whom God lays on your heart

♦encouraging and building others up in faith (Deuteronomy 3:28)

♦and finally serving others (Romans 12:10).

This scripture really captures the spirit of a minister.

"And whosoever will be chief (*protos*) among you, let him be your servant: {28} Even as the Son of man came not to be ministered unto, but to minister, and to give his life a ransom for many" (Matthew 20:27-28 KJV).

Remember there is an anointing provided for you the minister and we must never lose sight of the basic operations of that anointing. Jesus boldly declared, "The Spirit of the Lord is upon me, because he hath anointed me to preach the gospel to the poor; he hath sent me to heal the brokenhearted, to preach deliverance to the captives, and recovering of sight to the blind, to set at liberty them that are bruised, {19} To preach the acceptable year of the Lord" (Luke 4:18-19 KJV). The anointing has a definite purpose.

Here are six functions of the anointing...

1. Preach the gospel to the poor

2. Healing of the brokenhearted

3. Deliverance to captives

4. Sight to the blind

5. Liberty to those who are bruised (hurts and wounds)

6. God's favor (ministry of reconciliation)

Ministries are fueled by fervent prayer. In the next chapter we will examine the prayer life-style of the righteous that produces effective results.

Notes

[1]Jonas Clark, "Come Out!," (Hallandale, FL. Spirit of Life Publications, 2001)

CHAPTER 9

FERVENT PRAYER

There is a time to pray quietly and privately, but there is also a time to pray fervently and corporately. The apostolic equipping dimension will release a spirit of prayer into your life.

Y ou can expect upon entering the apostolic equipping dimension that your prayer life will be strongly affected. Prayer is the breeding ground for apostolic assignments. It is the realm of intimate communication and fellowship toward our Lord. Prayer is talking to God and him talking to you. In the apostolic dimension you will quickly learn that prayer is not something that you do but rather is the lifestyle of the righteous.

A prayer lifestyle is a consistent, integrated way of living.

The apostolic dimension will lead you into a realm of effective fervent targeted prayers that are guided by the Holy Spirit. The word teaches us that, "The effectual fervent prayer of a righteous man availeth much" (James 5:16 KJV). From this scripture we learn that there is a way that the righteous should pray in order to avail.

> To avail in prayer means to have
> great success.

The Amplified Bible teaches us through that same scripture that there is a tremendous power available for the righteous who pray fervently. Let's take a look.

> "The earnest (heartfelt, continued) prayer of a righteous man makes tremendous power available [dynamic in its working]" (James 5:16 AMP).

Are you ready for a tremendous prayer life? So what is fervent prayer? This scripture gives us a mighty key that unlocks a realm that few enter. It teaches us how to pray, get answers and releases tremendous power into our lives. Even Jesus' apostles did not know how to pray. They even asked the Lord to teach them how. We too must learn how to become effective in our prayer lives.

To pray with fervency means to pray with an emotional intensity. A fervent prayer is...

hot

burning

glowing

aggressive

strong

forceful

targeted

If you could pray the way Jesus did, would you? Jesus himself prayed fervently. The word teaches us,

> "Who in the days of his flesh, when he had offered up prayers and supplications with *strong crying* and tears unto him that was able to save him from death, and was heard in that he feared" (Hebrews 5:7 KJV, Italics added).

Notice that Jesus prayed while on the earth with strong crying mixed with tears.

The word strong is the Greek word *ischuros* meaning to be...

    loud

    powerful

    violent

    militant

    forcible

    strong

This is a picture of Jesus' personal prayer life that seldom is taught. Many people pray religiously. They go through a routine that is boring, lifeless, and ineffective. Jesus teaches us how he broke through in prayer. Let us learn from him.

There is a time to pray quietly and privately, but there is also a time to pray fervently and corporately. The apostolic equipping dimension will release a spirit of prayer into your life. Teaching out of her wonderful book, *Effective Fervent Prayer*, Mary Alice Isleib says,

"Jesus is coming soon. If we don't pray, who will? There is still much work to do, more

ground to break and prepare,
more enemies to defeat, battles
to win, strongholds to pull
down, and more of the plan of
God to be birthed in the earth.
'Your will be done on earth as it
is in heaven.'

PRAYER IS THE BREEDING GROUND FOR APOSTOLIC ASSIGNMENTS

We are living in a time that is
special; it's also a time where
the Church will be required to
pray as never before. When you
understand what prayer is and
how it works, you can see great
changes in your life and in your
city and nation. You can pray!
Jesus in you is a great Prayer
Warrior — He knows how and
what to pray to bring results.
He has given you His Word and
His Spirit. You are mighty in
Him! The Church holds the
keys to God's plan in the earth.
Prayer unlocks the door to God's

power in your personal life and
to deliverance for the nations."[1]

David Yonggi Cho, pastor of the largest
church in the world, the Yoida Full Gospel
Church in Soeul Korea, which has over a
million members, tells us how important
prayer is. "You could remove the powerful
preaching from our church and it would still
continue. You could remove the administra-
tion of pastoral care through the cell group
system and the church would still continue.
But if you removed the prayer life of our
church, it would collapse."[2]

The apostolic dimension will release you
into times of loud, strong, fervent, targeted,
effective prayer. Remember, fervent heartfelt
prayer is the key to an effective prayer life
and makes much of God's tremendous power
available. It is the power in prayer that will
shake the nations.

Next we will explore the wisdom of God
as he reveals to us his various apostolic
methods and strategies to build his church.

Notes
[1] Mary Alice Isleib, "Effective Fervent Prayer," (Minneapolis,
MI. Mary Alice Isleib Ministries, 1991), Preface.
2 Jim Williams, "Seoul Secrets," June 1989, P. 8).

CHAPTER 10

APOSTOLIC METHODS AND STRATEGIES

God is giving us effective strategies tailored for specific regions, territories and nations. He is the God of strategies and we can expect him to teach us how to succeed.

Many apostolic leaders are quickly discovering that what brought ministry success in years past is no longer working. Yesterday's methods for effective ministry are quickly failing. What's happening? We are in a time of transition and change. With the restoration of apostolic ministry is the restoration of apostolic methods and strategies. God is giving us effective strategies tailored for specific regions, territories, and nations. He is the God of strategies and we can expect him to teach us how to succeed.

Different territories may require different methods, tactics, and strategies. Let's take a look at China, compare it to the West, and see how God gives various strategies to reach various regions.

Did you know that 1/3 of the world population is in China (1,210,000,000)? Did you also know that in China there are no...

Christian television programs

Christian radio programs

churches painted white with big steeples

city wide gospel crusades

church meetings as we have in the West?

Did you know that Judaism and Christianity are strictly forbidden and against the law? Did you also know that there is an active aggression against Christianity? The prime target seems to be house church leaders who have refused to register with the Chinese government. Many are sentenced to three years "reeducation" in labor camps for the sole offense of carrying out peaceful religious activities.

Bureau officials regularly extort money from Christians by arresting them and refusing to release them until they pay a fine. They are often beaten in front of their families to force their relatives to pay the fines even though most are poor farmers with few or no resources.

China also requires all Christian churches to register by law with the government. After registration they then become subject to a string of restrictions affecting the selection and training of pastors, where they meet, what they can publish, their finances and their relations with believers overseas. Even certain preaching topics have been declared illegal including...

the second coming of Jesus

judgment day

the gifts of the Holy Spirit

creation

abortion

Registered churches are also barred from working with young people under the age of eighteen. Any believer who can't accept these government restrictions are driven underground. Their meetings are broken up, their property confiscated and their churches pulled down. Those who are arrested face fines, detention, and torture. Believers are beaten, hanged by the limbs, bound in excruciatingly painful positions, tormented with electric batons, and subjected to relentless interrogation. Many have even died under the beatings.

It was reported that there were official directives circulating in Heilongjiang Province setting out six religious rules:

1. Those under age 18 cannot be evangelized.

2. No government staff can embrace a faith.

3. No military staff can embrace a faith.

4. No students or teachers can embrace a faith.

5. All religious activity must be carried out in an approved venue.

6. No foreigners can preach without government approval.

Yet in spite of all these persecutions the house church in China is currently estimated to be between 30 and 100 million strong.

GOD OF STRATEGIES

How could it be possible for God to reach a nation with such a high level of opposition? Obviously the Western paradigm of drawing people to a building would not be an effective strategy for reaching the lost in China. The Chinese church would need some different strategies. Remember, "But unto every one of us is given grace according to the measure *(metron)* of the gift of Christ" (Ephesians 4:7 KJV).

YESTERDAY'S METHODS
FOR EFFECTIVE MINISTRY
ARE QUICKLY FAILING

A friend of mine returning from China told me of an interesting strategy in regards to evangelism that I wanted to pass on to you. As you know Christianity and Judaism are outlawed in China and it is illegal to freely assemble in worship and have church like we do in the West. With that in mind you can see that God would have to give the Chinese people a different strategy to reach their nation. One of the strategies that I heard dealt with *families* taking upon themselves the responsibility to promote the gospel.

91

When a family becomes born again in China some interesting things take place. They immediately seek the baptism of the Holy Spirit, then the spirit of prayer and evangelism comes over the people. I have been told that you can see a visible passion on the people.

Because Christianity is illegal and people gather for church in their homes, the family appoints one family member as an evangelist. Then anoints and sends that family member out in full time evangelistic service. That family member has no other job outside of reaching the lost. The other family members then take upon themselves the responsibility of financially supporting the family evangelist. Although I *strongly* promote the priesthood of all believers throughout this book I am fascinated by this unique strategy.

MIGRATION EVANGELISM

Another strategy being promoted is migration evangelism. Some underground churches are beginning to network with one another and are quickly training preachers to start their own churches in other villages throughout China. Some practice migration evangelism by moving couples to remote provinces to live as business people while at the same time trying to influence their neighbors.

92

These radical evangelist say that the only hope in changing China is not by revolution but by the changing of the hearts of the people in the nation. They believe that once the nation is full of Christian lawyer's, teachers, postal workers, etc., then true change will take place.

One might think with all the opposition against the church in China that the believers would tend to grow weary, become lukewarm and give up, but quite the contrary is happening. The Chinese believe that without persecution and obstacles they might lose their fire. They carry such a zeal for God that they not only want a person to come to Christ, but entire cities and finally their country. I think the Western church could benefit extremely from such a passionate view of ministry.

The point of this chapter is that God will give us three things to succeed in our *metrons* regardless of where our ministries are located. They are...

♦ wisdom

♦ grace

♦ effective strategies

When you enter the apostolic dimension, regardless of what city or nation you are in,

93

God will give you various methods and strategies to accomplish your calling.

In the next chapter we are going to take a look at the importance of apostolic teams and small groups and the nuts and bolts of a structural change.

CHAPTER 11

THE HARVEST STRATEGY

More than any other structure, apostolic teams and small groups give every person a way to minister their gifts. Apostolic teams take the church out of the building and into the city.

Teams and small groups are the future of apostolic churches. In today's society it is impossible for one pastor to meet the complex needs of every individual in a church. God's answer to ministering to one another is through the restoration of the truth of the priesthood of every believer.

More than any other structure, apostolic teams and small groups give *every* person a way to minister their gifts. Apostolic teams take the church out of the building and into the city. Small groups multiply the number of ministers in a given church. These small groups (cells) also close the back door of the church as precious people fall through the cracks never to be seen again.

Operating in the priesthood of a believer will manifest itself in a love for and ministry to one another (1 John 3:11; 4:7, 11-12).

Apostolic ministry is not confined to a building. The building is only the center or base of ministry operations. It is not the culmination of our calling to only fill such a building. Our calling is to...

> invade and occupy our cities
> with the gospel of Jesus Christ
>
> to be disciple makers of disciple
> makers

Just as we saw the effectiveness of small groups in China we will see the power and effectiveness of apostolic teams and small groups in the emerging apostolic churches of the 21st Century.

So having said much in this book about the restoration of the priesthood of every believer (every Christian is a minister), how can we begin to change the structure of the local church from a one-man-only paradigm into a fully mobilized army of believers? My admonition is that we can change the structure of the local church and create a pattern whereby everyone who is available can minister. Let's look at one strategy for some ideas on how to transition into a fully functional apostolic ministry.

THE STRUCTURE

One day while in prayer for strategies and wisdom to be effective in ministry I received a vision of a net that I saw stretched out across the world and in our city. I also heard the Holy Spirit say, "I am building a great net for a great catch." Along with the vision of this net the Holy Spirit gave me a strategy of apostolic teams and small groups invading and occupying — *metrons*. Again, the Greek word *metron* means an assigned place of spiritual jurisdiction (2 Corinthians 10:13).

APOSTOLIC TEAMS

At Spirit of Life Ministries church where I am the "set man" (Numbers 27:16) we believe in the Biblical concept of apostolic teams. You can learn more about apostolic teams by reading my book, *"Governing Churches and Antioch Apostles."1* In this book I go into detail about the function of apostolic street teams that have been trained to be effective in ministry. Basically an apostolic team...

> is a group of sons and daughters of the ministry who work together and are sent forth out of the local church with a specific assignment and a common

cause. They are an invading
task force.

Apostolic teams benefit from the apostolic dynamic of being sent forth (*apo-stello*)
out of the local church (Acts 13:3). The apostolic team consists of people who are willing and available to go onto the streets to
evangelize.

Apostolic street teams are used
to reach the lost, the unchurched, and start metron
groups (cells) throughout the
city.

These metron groups represent the knots
in the net that I prophetically saw. Becoming part of an apostolic team is the entry
point for being a part of the church's exciting apostolic dimension. As part of a team
one can be trained in leadership, evangelism and how to work with others. As one
proves faithful in the work and takes own-
ership of the vision of reaching the city with
the gospel of Jesus Christ they are then eli-
gible to advance as a Metron Leader.

METRON LEADERS

A Metron Leader is one who leads a cell
group of at least three people and no more

than ten. The goal of a Metron Leader is to raise up leaders in a small group setting outside the church. In effect they are...

disciple makers of disciple makers.

The Metron Leader's lifetime goal is to train 12 other Metron Leaders and help them pioneer and plant 12 other cell groups.[2] A Metron Leader in addition to meeting weekly with his metron group outside the church also meets with his group of 12 Metron Leaders at least once per month.

Metron Leaders must themselves become Master Builders. We encourage every Metron Leader at the church to multiply their metron group every 6 months. The maximum time to multiply a metron group is every 12 months. Metron groups that do not multiply are absorbed into other metron groups. Metron groups must be mobilized to evangelize.

METRON GROUPS

Metron groups (cells) meet weekly in homes for the purpose of fellowship, discipleship, and setting goals to multiply. In this setting the Metron Leader can, in an intimate way, give personal ministry and help fulfill the specific needs of the group. A typical metron group meeting consist of personal and corporate prayer, worship, lesson, offering, etc. The main focus of the metron group is four-fold. They are...

♦ evangelism

♦ discipleship

♦ multiplication

♦ leadership training

It is imperative that every member of the metron group be able to understand and repeat these three parts of the metrons vision when asked. Metron groups assume responsibility in reaching their family, friends and neighborhoods. The role of the Metron Leader is that of a nurturing care giver who attends more closely to the groups needs and personal ministry.

> Apostolic street teams coupled with various evangelistic events is the *invasion* strategy of an apostolic ministry into the city. Whereas metron groups (cells) is the *occupying* strategy of an apostolic ministry into the city.

THE INVASION COUNCIL

Every Metron Leader is then allowed a seat on the city's Invasion Council. This apostolic council's focus is leadership training, growth, and evangelism. The Invasion Council is made up of Metron Leaders only. This group meets together monthly in a leadership session in prayer to set and evaluate goals as well as strategies. The Invasion Council is under the direction of the set man and the oversight of the church's apostolic presbytery.

TEAMS AND SMALL GROUPS
ARE THE FUTURE OF
APOSTOLIC MINISTRIES

Invasion Counsel membership is based solely on merit and hard work. It is a worthy and attainable goal.

MASTER BUILDER

A Master Builder is a metron leader who has discipled 12 other metron leaders and helped them start metron groups.

When you multiply leaders who multiply leaders the result will be many metron

101

(cell) groups under your care. A Master Builder has reached his goal of developing a team of 12 leaders. A Master Builder meets with their group of 12 Metron Leaders a minimum of once per month to establish goals and evaluate their progress.

Once a Metron Leader helps 12 others become Metron Leaders he then advances to the position of Master Builder. Becoming a Master Builder through the apostolic structure is a position of honor that is reached only because of hard work, perseverance and dedication in advancing the gospel throughout the city.

In the next chapter we will discuss the crucial need for apostolic leadership development and some of the basic requirements needed.

Notes

1 Jonas Clark, "Governing Churches And Antioch Apostles," (Hallandale, FL. Spirit of Life Publications, 2001)

2 The groups of 12 concept can be read about in "Groups of 12" by Joel Comiskey, (Houston TX, Touch Publications, 1999)

CHAPTER 12

LEADERSHIP TRAINING

Jesus is our pattern for the greatest of all apostolic leaders. He took twelve ordinary men with various personalities, weaknesses, flaws and strengths and transformed them into a dynamic, world changing revolutionary team.

The apostolic equipping dimension along with the restoration of the priesthood of all believers paints a bright future for the 21st Century church. Yet to achieve the transitional changes necessary will be an exciting challenge to the emerging apostolic ministries. To accomplish this great strategy and enter the apostolic equipping dimension will require a focus on leadership training. As a church implements an apostolic structure they will promptly find out that the harvest is truly plenteous, but the labor's (leaders) are few.

Leadership development will quickly take center stage as our greatest need in our efforts to advance the gospel and build strong apostolic governing churches. For believers to take leadership seriously they must be in the presence of those who take leadership seriously.

The skills required to become an apostolic leader don't come overnight. They are developed in the hard knocks of ministry as we move forward in our callings. It has been said that an overnight success really took ten years. It takes time and practice to mold and shape leadership skills. What you practice you get better at. We will have to become masters at training new apostolic leaders within our churches. So what is apostolic leadership?

> Leadership in its simplest form is the ability to accomplish a purpose by recruiting and motivating others to join a common cause. Apostolic leadership in particular recognizes the importance of a strong governing local church, embraces the apostolic sent one dynamics, is a team player, spiritually equips and deploys every believer.

Jesus is our pattern for the greatest of all apostolic leaders. He took twelve ordinary men with various personalities, weakness, flaws and strengths and transformed them into a dynamic, world changing revolutionary team.

A strong desire is essential to becoming an apostolic leader but by itself is insufficient. One must learn and practice the skills necessary to obtain success. How many of the following leadership qualities do you have. Apostolic leaders are...

VISIONARIES — Vision is like a compass. It identifies and sets the direction and the course of things. Without the ability to see there can be no action.

COMMITTED — Leaders are dedicated and devoted to a long term course of action and involvement.

EFFECTIVE COMMUNICATORS — Communication is the act of transmitting information in a clear and concise way. Apostolic leaders are masters of building faith for action through effective communication.

GOAL SETTERS — Goals are targets. They are defined as the line or place at which a race or trip is ended. Goals breakdown a leaders vision into small attainable steps.

RISK TAKERS — All apostolic leaders must enter the realm of uncharted territories of risk. This is faith in action. They are willing to try what has never been tried before.

RESULTS ORIENTED — Apostolic leaders "take hold" and get the job done — period!

AGENTS OF CHANGE — Apostolic leaders are the instruments of change who act as the stimulus in bringing about and hastening results. To them, simply to talk about necessary changes without an active plan of reform is sin.

INITIATORS — Apostolic leaders are the instigators and activist of action. They step forward, take charge, are willing to act while coming up with solutions and ideas on their own.

PERSEVERANT — Perseverance is a steady persistence in a course of action in spite of difficulties, obstacles or discouragement. Apostolic leaders are master overcomers. To overcome means to win the struggle and carry off the victory.

LIFE LONG LEARNERS — Apostolic leaders are avid readers who are into continual self development by learning from mistakes, failures and successes of themselves and others. Emerging apostolic leaders can be identified by the books and teaching cassettes in their personal libraries. One becomes what they pursue.

ADULTS — Apostolic leaders are mature and ready to take leadership responsibility seriously.

FLEXIBLE AND FLUID — Apostolic leaders are willing to try and experiment with new and unproven ways of achieving results. They have the ability to adapt to the situation they are currently in. Because they are fluid they can move and change shape without separating under pressure.

DECISIVE — Apostolic leaders are decisive, they have the ability to speedily examine a situation, settle a question or dispute, and make rapid and accurate decisions.

TEAM PLAYERS — Apostolic leaders know how to work with others. They realize that it takes a team to accomplish a great vision. They cannot do all that needs to be done by themselves.

This is a short list of leadership attributes. How did you rate yourself? Did you see these qualities in yourself? I encourage every reader to study leadership skills. Study the word of God and learn from others who have done what you are trying to do. If you haven't started building a personal leadership library, make a decision to start one today. Remember this thought — 'every reader is not a leader, but every leader is a reader.'

I want to share an advertisement that British Antarctic explorer Sir Ernest Shackleton (1874-1922) placed in the London newspapers in 1900 in preparation for the National Antarctic Expedition (which subsequently failed to reach the South Pole). This ad so captures the adventurous spirit of apostolic leadership that it is a fitting conclusion to this chapter.

> MEN WANTED FOR HAZARD-OUS JOURNEY. Small wages, bitter cold, long months of complete darkness, constant danger, safe return doubtful. Honor and recognition in case of success.
> Ernest Shackleton.[1]

Shackleton later said that after placing this ad for volunteers, "it seemed as though all of Great Britain were determined to accompany me, the response was so overwhelming."

If Shackleton evoked such a great response for his cause with a simple newspaper ad, what kind of response can our Lord expect for His cause?

> ## APOSTOLIC LEADERS ARE THE
> ## INSTIGATORS AND ACTIVIST OF ACTION

In the next chapter we will look at the effect of the apostolic dimension on music.

Notes

[1] William J. Bennett, "The Book of Virtues," (New York NY.)

CHAPTER 13

MUSIC FOR
AN APOSTOLIC GENERATION

What makes apostolic worship so different is not necessarily the music itself but rather the spiritual realm that it takes you into. That realm has more 'punch in the praise' and more 'depth in the worship.'

The apostolic dimension will take you into a realm of worship and sound that perhaps you have not been familiar with. Why? Because every fresh move of God has its own music and songs. So too in this emerging apostolic generation. Since the apostolic anointing is foundational to the church we can expect to see continual change take place in the presentation, function, flow and sound of music in apostolic churches around the world. Because of the subjective nature of worship music and style, it is not easy to explain what apostolic worship is all about. I am sure that there are many others who can articulate the subject much better so I will only list some of my observations on the subject.

FERVENT LIFESTYLE OF WORSHIP

Not only does the apostolic equipping dimension release a fervent prayer life in every believer, it also imparts a fervent lifestyle of worship. When apostolic believers gather together in a corporate celebration something powerful takes place. There is an entrance into another realm. Immediately you can feel the spiritual climate beckoning you to move out of being a passive spectator into a vibrant participant.

What makes apostolic worship so different is not necessarily the music itself but rather the spiritual realm that it takes you to. That realm has more 'punch in the praise' and more 'depth in the worship.' Like a bus, the music is really only a vehicle that the Holy Spirit uses to transport you from one place to another. You can stand gazing at a bus, choose to get in it or not. You can sit in the bus alone or with many others. Or you might only watch others drive the bus and refuse to drive it yourself. Music is only the vehicle that the Holy Spirit uses to transport you.

MUSICS' INFLUENCE

Music has an incredible influence on people when it is filled with spiritual substance and purpose. God created us as beings of worship. Music belongs to God and is a powerful medium of the Holy Spirit. Music itself was created for one central purpose, to celebrate and worship the King of Kings and the Lord of Lords.

Apostolic worship is not a style or type of music, but a means to bring one to a powerful and often life-influencing encounter with God. It is experienced in the Spirit of life that emanates throughout the music. In other words, apostolic worship sets the stage for creative expression that can often be seen through emotional reactions of fervent jubilation by those who have entered in.

The changing nature of the apostolic dimension is progressively affecting music in a big way. We must not forget that music is a vehicle of worship. As the church matures in the apostolic dimension so this 'vehicle' and its influence will become increasingly more powerful in its affect in people's lives.

> Musical worship at its core is simply an expression of our love, adoration, and intimate devotion of God through the music and songs. Whereas

songs are the spoken declaration of that devotion, music is the vehicle of that expression.

The apostolic expression in music will move you into another realm. It's a place of vibrant gestures and even prophetic expression. It's not just about feelings either, but it's about purpose. Apostolic music is alive! There are churches who attempt to be more relevant and up to date with their worship music by playing contemporary songs. However, just copying another form or model is not enough. There will be no expression of an apostolic dimension if they or the congregation are only 'watching' and not actively engaged in worship themselves. They are then only entertaining those who are watching, and any real activity in the Spirit realm will be negligible. What is really needed is an apostolic revelation in the church and in those who are ministering, then the music, the songs and the participation will follow.

NEW SONGS

Apostolic worship is the breeding ground of new songs that address the specific needs of your church or the body of Christ. For example, the Holy Spirit birthed a new song in our church. The words in the chorus said this, "I hear a shout in the distance saying come up higher." This song was definitely the Holy Spirit speaking to us about coming up higher in our worship and coming closer in our relationship with him. It was prophetic instruction for us to take another step closer in our walk with the Lord.

APOSTOLIC MUSIC PREPARES THE SPIRITUAL CLIMATE

Sometimes songs birthed in a local church in an apostolic atmosphere have a universal application in the broad body of Christ. Because of the governing authority in apostolic churches the songs are relevant to many other churches as well.

The apostolic dimension will birth new songs appropriate and relevant to your churches current situation. Singing songs to the Lord is the most powerful way to worship our Lord.

The Holy Spirit will use a company of worshippers to birth new songs that powerfully affect the entire church and take them to another level in the Spirit. One could liken it to a spiritual upgrade. This spiritual upgrade should be our goal because it is a genuinely exciting place to be in as a church.

115

Not only are you building something powerful in the realm of the spirit, you are releasing something powerful in the lives of the people, too.

CULTURAL INFLUENCES

Music style is progressive and often determined by one's culture. However we must not confuse culture with the apostolic dimension. For example Latin churches may have a different sound than Caribbean Island churches or even African churches, but the apostolic dimension moves all people into a realm of effectiveness in worship in regards to...

intimate worship

high praises

prophetic decrees

spiritual warfare

The difference is not the cultural sound, but the apostolic dimension flowing in that sound.

DIFFERENT FLOWS

There are many different flows in modern Christian music like Vineyard, Integrity,
116

Maranatha, Hillsongs, Black Gospel, Messianic, and many others. There is also emerging an apostolic music that is just as identifiable but perhaps not as easily labeled. It will never be confused with worldliness but will take people to another realm in the Spirit. The apostolic dimension is as the scripture tells us "deep calling unto deep." It is undeniable and reaches right into our hearts while transporting us into the presence of God.

HUMANISM IN WORSHIP

The apostolic dimension will challenge and break you out of a self-centered worship life-style. Many only worship God in hopes of being ministered to by him. Of course God ministers to his people and refreshes them as they worship him. However the Holy Spirit wants to refresh us, rearm us and prepare us to live a victorious Christian life.

The apostolic equipping dimension will challenge one to come up higher in every way and to stop worshipping God out of a spirit of humanism, self-promotion or even self-centeredness. Apostolic worship is not about bless-me-only. I have seen people with hurts, wounds and rejection try to use worship as a hiding place. They often seek a worship experience that brings a temporary

117

refreshing without deliverance. You can see them resist high praise because they do not understanding that the anointing in the apostolic dimension will set you free from your past and launch you powerfully into your future.

WORSHIP LEADERS

In apostolic worship the Holy Spirit, not the worship leader is in control of the service. As the worship leader yields himself to the moving of the Holy Spirit, the Spirit himself administrates the worship service. Whether it be times of quiet reverence, high praises or of militant spiritual warfare. As in 2 Chronicles 5:11-14, they all made *one sound* and the glory filled the house and took over the meeting.

UNPREDICTABLE

Apostolic worship is often unpredictable. Even though there is initially a time frame involved the Holy Spirit has the freedom to change that time. To extend or even to shorten the worship part of a service is up to him. Futher we see in 2 Chronicles 5:13 they sang "For He is good and His mercy endures forever" and that was it the Holy Ghost took over!

Ture apostolic musicians understand their roles as being worshippers first and musicians last. Their love for Jesus supersedes their love for music. These ministers of music will usher in God's glory in these final days.

EXPRESSION

Apostolic worship is often mixed with shouts of praise, lifted up hands, clapping, cries of heart wrenching passionate worship, and exuberant dancing. There is a solid connection and interaction between the worshipper and the Holy Spirit. The songs and the music really *move* you. There are times in the service when there is a collective synergy among the worshippers.

According to my Australian friend, Prophet Stephen Bennett, this synergy is what some musicians call "being in the pocket." In that place it seems that the Lord himself is in our midst and worship becomes a targeted release to him. Apostolic worship reveals the majesty, glory, grandeur and worthiness of God. Apostolic worship is not a style or type of music but rather a vibrant lively demonstration of intimacy. It is the place where apostolic power ultimately has its beginnings.

PROPHETIC DIMENSION

Apostolic worship takes you into the prophetic realms of the Holy Spirit that you
cannot get to outside the apostolic dimension. It provides a platform for a release of
strong prophetic decrees that minister to the
Lord or minister to the current need of the
local church. Prophecy and apostolic worship are inseparable. Oftentimes the worship service will move into prophetic songs
that had never been played before.

"Moreover David and the cap-
tains of the host separated to
the service of the sons of Asaph,
and of Heman, and of
Jeduthun, *who should proph-
esy with harps, with psalteries,
and with cymbals*" (1
Chronicles 25:1 KJV, Italics
added).

HEALING AND DELIVERANCE

Scripture is clear that there is a realm in
music that sets the stage for healing and
deliverance. When King Saul was being tormented by evil spirits David played music
and Saul was freed, healed and refreshed.

"Let our lord now command thy servants, which are before thee, to seek out a man, who is a cunning player on an harp: and it shall come to pass, when the evil spirit from God is upon thee, that he shall play with his hand, and thou shalt be well" (1 Samuel 16:16).

"And it came to pass, when the evil spirit from God was upon Saul, that David took an harp, and played with his hand: so Saul was refreshed, and was well, and the evil spirit departed from him" (1 Samuel 16:23).

WHAT APOSTOLIC WORSHIP DOES

Apostolic worship is not just a place of restoration and refreshing or a place where one can feel good and hide out, but a place to be refreshed, equipped, released, and sent out. Apostolic worship will minister to the Lord, release prophetic decrees, bring refreshing and healing. But it can also be militant and warfare-like while challenging the hardness of the spiritual climate of the meeting. Apostolic worship literally takes you into the presence of God and prepares one's heart for the release of the word of God. It also sets the tone or the atmosphere of the meeting. Let's look at some of the things that apostolic worship does.

1. MOVES THE GLORY

> "And David danced before the LORD with all his might; and David was girded with a linen ephod. {15} So David and all the house of Israel brought up the ark of the LORD with shouting, and with the sound of the trumpet" (2 Samuel 6:14-15 KJV).

Apostolic worship moves the glory of God from one place to another. We can look at the life of King David as a type of apostolic restoration in worship. King David entered an apostolic dimension when he took off his kingly robes of position and status, and danced before the Lord. This expression of his love and dedication literally moved the glory of God from Obededom's house to Jerusalem. We can do the same as we humble ourselves and flow with what the Lord is doing in this apostolic hour in the church.

2. WARRING IN WORSHIP

There is also a strong warring spirit in the apostolic dimension of worship. I remember a song that said, "teach us to war in our worship." This song was teaching the body of Christ to learn that the Holy Spirit could use music as a spiritual weapon to war against spiritual forces who were attacking the church. The word is clear that as we worship our God he sets ambushes against our enemies.

When under siege Jehoshaphat appointed holy singers to praise the Lord. While they were praising God he set ambushes against their enemies. The apostolic dimension releases us into this realm.

> "And Jehoshaphat bowed his head with his face to the ground: and all Judah and the inhabitants of Jerusalem fell before the LORD, worshipping the LORD. {19} And the Levites, of the children of the Kohathites, and of the children of the Korhites, stood up to praise the LORD God of Israel with a loud voice on high. {20} And they rose early in the morning, and went forth into the wilderness of Tekoa: and as they went

123

forth, Jehoshaphat stood and said, Hear me, O Judah, and ye inhabitants of Jerusalem; Believe in the LORD your God, so shall ye be established; believe his prophets, so shall ye prosper. {21} And when he had consulted with the people, he appointed singers unto the LORD, and that should praise the beauty of holiness, as they went out before the army, and to say, Praise the LORD; for his mercy endureth for ever. {22} *And when they began to sing and to praise, the LORD set ambushments* against the children of Ammon, Moab, and mount Seir, which were come against Judah; and they were smitten" (2 Chronicles 20:18-22 KJV Italics added).

3. SEPARATES, EQUIPS AND SENDS

In the Antioch church, before there was an apostolic team released the people are seen ministering (worshipping) the Lord (Acts 13:1-2). In that atmosphere of worship the Holy Ghost was moved to speak and give the church instructions and assignments.

Today, too the Lord has assignments of

sound for your church, your city and nation. As you flow in the apostolic dimension of what the Lord is restoring today and become equipped as 'governing people' you will begin to experience the excitement of genuine powerful ongoing change by the Holy Spirit that will bear much fruit in the lives of people.

In the next chapter we will take a look at the apostolic frontier — the nations.

CHAPTER 14

INTO THE NATIONS

*The apostolic anointing will produce a
heart for the nations. The word tells us that
after the power of the Holy Spirit is come
upon us that we will be witnesses of Jesus
both in our hometowns and even unto the
uttermost parts of the earth (Acts 1:8).*

The nations are the apostolic frontier.
There are many who talk about the
nations, but you will never have any
interest in reaching the nations until God
imparts into you a heart for them. The Bible
says that all nations shall come and worship him (Revelation 15:4). The apostolic dimension is a realm whereby all races, cul-
tures, tribes, and nations are gathered together to worship their God. The apostolic
dimension causes one to look upon the
fields that are white and ready for harvest.
This dimension will give you a compelling
earnest desire to reach the nations of the
world with the saving gospel of Jesus Christ.

In fact a vision for the nations is *the* apostolic mandate.

THE NATIONS
ARE THE APOSTOLIC FRONTIER

"Ask of me, and I shall give thee the heathen for thine inheritance, and the uttermost parts of the earth for thy possession" (Psalm 2:8 KJV).

The apostolic anointing will produce a heart for the nations. The word tells us that after the power of the Holy Spirit is come upon us that we will be witnesses of Jesus both in our hometowns and even unto the uttermost parts of the earth (Acts 1:8). As previously mentioned, the Greek word for witness is *martus,* meaning — to make known the record and to bear the testimony.

The word *martus* is also where we get the English word martyred. This speaks of one with such a powerful testimony that they are willing to die for it's advancement.

Currently the Holy Spirit is networking together emerging apostolic centers around the world. Are you ready to enter the apostolic frontier? When a church embraces the ministry of apostles then the sending dimension of that anointing will be released in its midst. When that happens you can expect some real structural changes to take place such as...

♦ a challenge of religious structures that have focused primarily on nurturing the existing church members

♦ a transition from a one-man-only ministry structure to the formation of apostolic teams

♦ prophetic insight and decrees

♦ an upgrade in spiritual authority

♦ activation of spiritual government

♦ an alignment of prayer with the apostolic structure

♦ a panoramic view of the church rather than a local view only

129

♦ apostolic function and name will begin to match up

♦ targeting of territories and nations for the release of apostolic teams

♦ a focus on planting and building strong apostolic centers worldwide

After reading this book I pray that you have received some helpful insight into the direction of apostolic ministry and the dynamic of the apostolic equipping dimension. Although we don't have all the answers at least we are being obedient to walk out what we have thus far. I am captivated with the continual unfolding plan of God as he demonstrates his great wisdom as The Master Apostolic Leader. What an exciting time to be alive!

When I finished writing this chapter something strange and quite unusual happened to me, the Spirit of God gave me a poem. So I thought it fitting to end with it.

APOSTLES' ONE
by Jonas Clark

To Christ the nations beckon come,
the revolution now begun.

Who will hearken His mighty call,
to see a world to him be drawn?

Rise up ye mighty apostles' one,
for Jesus Christ himself will come.

From days of old to now we've come,
have seen great blessings now begun.

Will strength prevail this too unveil?
Will hope rise up this hour avail?

Me thinkest His Word of truth prevail,
Rise up ye mighty apostles' one.

His church be built without question one,
Stand strong this hour His victory won!

APPENDIX A

Sola gratia, by grace alone

"For by grace are ye saved through faith; and that not of yourselves: it is the gift of God: {9} Not of works, lest any man should boast" (Ephesians 2:8-9 KJV).

"But we believe that through the grace of the Lord Jesus Christ we shall be saved, even as they" (Acts 15:11 KJV).

Sola fide, through faith alone

"Therefore being justified by faith, we have peace with God through our Lord Jesus Christ: {2} By whom also we have access by faith into this grace wherein we stand, and rejoice in hope of the glory of God" (Romans 5:1-2 KJV).

"Knowing that a man is not justified by the works of the law, but by the faith of Jesus Christ, even we have believed in Jesus Christ, that we might be justi fied by the faith of Christ, and not by the works of the law: for by the works of the law shall no flesh be justified" (Galations 2:16 KJV).

Sola Scriptura, according to scripture alone

"All scripture is given by inspiration of God, and is profitable for doctrine, for reproof, for correction, for instruction in righteousness: {17} That the man of God may be perfect, thoroughly furnished unto all good works" (2 Timothy 3:16-17 KJV).

"But though we, or an angel from heaven, preach any other gospel unto you than that which we have preached unto you than that which we have preached unto you, let him be accursed" (Galations 1:8 KJV).

Soli Deo Gloria, for God's Glory alone

"I am the LORD: that is my name: and my glory will I not give to another, neither my praise to graven images" (Isaiah 42:8 KJV).

"For God, who commanded the light to shine out of darkness, hath shined in our hearts, to give the light of the knowledge of the glory of God in the face of Jesus Christ" (2 Corinthians 4:6 KJV).

INVITATION

Hello friends and partners!

In addition to preaching the gospel around the world, we also have a powerful church in South Florida and would love to have you visit with us. The Spirit of God told us to start a church and raise up people in strength and power who would reach their city and impact the nations. SOLM has an international apostolic and prophetic call, as well as a mandate to raise up a strong local church by ministering to the whole family. SOLM has the reputation of being a place where you can receive what you need from the Lord; whether it be healing, miracles, deliverance, restoration, victory, or success. Why? Because with God all things are possible. SOLM' uniqueness is being recognized and sought after as we continue growing in spiritual liberty, influence, strength and power. We invite you to come and receive confirmation, impartation, and activation.

In the Master's service,
Jonas and Rhonda Clark

PROPHETIC OPERATIONS

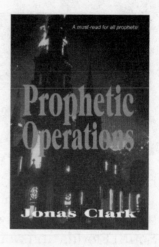

The prophets may give personal prophecies, but their revelation gifting goes way beyond personal prophecy. Power, money, prestige, honor, promotion, and enticements, with smooth flattering sayings, are all demonic assignments designed to pull on any common ground that might be in the heart of God's prophetic ministers.

Our society is filled with those who come into our churches who have formerly opened themselves up to new age mysticism, witchcraft, the occult, and spiritualism. To protect the flock from false anointings and familiar spirits, there is a proper order in which the Holy Spirit likes to flow.

It's time for accurate prophetic operations!

ISBN 1-886885-11-7

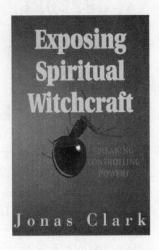

EXPOSING SPIRITUAL WITCHCRAFT

Spiritual witchcraft is the power of Satan. Its purpose is to control and manipulate you.

The weapons of witchcraft are emotional manipulation, spiritual and religious control, isolation, soul ties, fear, confusion, loss of personal identity, sickness, depression and prophetic divination.

Those caught in the snare of this spirit struggle all their Christian life to remain stable in their walk with Christ.

Topics include: the character of spiritual witchcraft, the weapons of witchcraft, the road to deception and lastly — breaking free!

"I fought this spirit from April to November and won. So can you!"

ISBN 1-886885-00-1

JEZEBEL SEDUCING GODDESS OF WAR

Jezebel is the warrior goddess who has gone unchallenged in our generation. Dr. Lester Sumrall said that she would be the greatest opposer of the apostolic church before the coming of the Lord. In 1933 Voice of Healing Prophet William Branham had a vision of her rising to take control.

"Some people write about things that they know nothing about. Not this time! It is time to barbecue this spirit."

ISBN 1-886885-04-4

50 EARMARKS OF AN APOSTOLIC CHURCH

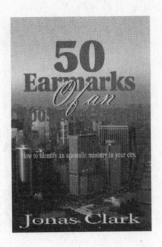

Jesus said, "I will build my church and the gates of hell shall not prevail." So what kind of church is it that Jesus is building? Is it a religious church? A traditional church? A defeated church? Or is it a glorious church without spot or wrinkle?

Right now we are experiencing an awesome paradigm shift in ministry. The Holy Spirit is moving us into a time of the restoration of the apostolic ministry. All over the world God is birthing apostolic churches. But what do they look like? What makes them so different? Is there one in your city? In this thought-provoking book Jonas teaches you 50 earmarks of an apostolic church in your city. It's time to cross the bridge into the apostolic. Are you ready to be a part of an exciting glorious church?

ISBN 1-886885-06-0

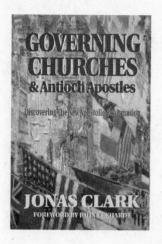

GOVERNING CHURCHES & ANTIOCH APOSTLES

Apostolic churches build, guide, govern, blast, establish, carry liberty, impart blessing, set, father, mature, set the pace, influence, train, send, launch, hear, say and do.

A new move of the Holy Spirit has begun! It is the call for a new apostolic reformation. This reformation is challenging old religious structures and systems. It is restoring the understanding of an apostolic church that will enable us to fulfill the great commission. It's time to discover your role in the new apostolic reformation.

ISBN 1-886885-07-9

IMAGINATIONS DON'T LIVE THERE!

Have you floated out into an imagination today? The Word of God teaches us to be led by the Spirit of God. However, we must first learn how to conquer the weird world of soulish imaginations. An imagination is a picture conceived in the spirit of one's mind that forms a mental picture of what is not. Imaginations speak of things that haven't happened and are not real. Once spoken they come alive. When acted on they lead to fear, instability, and feelings of insecurity. The freedom to imagine must first be fortified with truth. This book will help you take control of your mind and free you to be led by the Spirit of God.

ISBN 1-886885-03-6

COME OUT!

It is time for the church to exercise her authority against Satan who has been allowed to maintain his oppression without a challenge. In this handbook for the serious deliverance minister we will study...

the scriptural foundations for deliverance

how to continue the deliverance ministry of Jesus

the different types of spirits mentioned in the Bible

how to cast out devils

six things evil spirits attach themselves to

how to keep our deliverance

and much more.

ISBN 1-886885-10-0

RELIGIOUS SPIRITS

One of the most deadly influences in the body of Christ today is the religious spirit.

Religious people themselves have been used as the devil's assassins, targeting the spiritually young, the zealous, the hungry and the leadership.

This book will speak into the lives of those who are being spiritually abused by religious spirits who steal the spiritual zeal from God-called, anointed, and appointed children of God.

All of us have experienced the onslaught of the religious spirit in our lives. This book will open the eyes of those who themselves have been seduced into religious forms and traditions of men, and offer them a way out of carnal religious activity.

ISBN 1-886885-12-5

Global Cause Network

THE GLOBAL CAUSE NETWORK is a network of churches and ministries that have united together to build a platform for an apostolic voice. The *GCN* is built on relationships rather than denominational politics. It consists of those who recognize the importance of apostolic gifts working together with all five ascension gifts to equip believers for the work of ministry. By uniting we have forged an alliance across the globe that is building a 'great net for a great catch.' The foundational vision of the *GCN* is covenant relationships between its membership for the advancement of the gospel of Jesus Christ throughout the world.

MISSION STATEMENT

• To reach the world with the gospel of Jesus Christ.

• To build and strengthen the local church.

THE GLOBAL CAUSE NETWORK PROVIDES...

• apostolic and prophetic identity with a strong sense of community

• a platform to coordinate, enhance and release God's apostolic and prophetic voice

• a focus to impact our cities and the nations with the gospel

• apostolic covering, confirmation, impartation, activation, team ministry, sending, church planting and release of ministry gifts

• critical learning resources, educational and informational materials vital to the advancement of the network

• apostolic fathering, focus and direction

• facilitation of relationship by connecting those of like precious faith together

For more information contact the GCN ministry office.

The Global Cause Network
Apostle Jonas Clark
27 West Hallandale Beach Blvd
Hallandale, Florida
33009
(954) 456-4420

email: life@catchlife.org
Web site www.catchlife.org

MINISTRY INFORMATION

For a complete ministry catalog of tapes, books and videos, or to invite Jonas to speak at your next conference, please contact

Spirit of Life Ministries
27 West Hallandale Beach Blvd.
Hallandale, Florida 33009
(954) 456-4420

email: life@catchlife.org

BOOKS
BY JONAS CLARK

Jezebel, Seducing Goddess of War

Exposing Spiritual Witchcraft

Apostolic Equipping Dimension

Come Out!

Governing Churches & Antioch Apostles

50 Earmarks of an Apostolic Church

Imaginations, Don't Live There!

Prophetic Operations

Religious Spirits

Available in
quality Christian bookstores or
easy on-line internet ordering
http://catchlife.org or call toll free
(800) 943-6490

Spirit of Life Ministries
27 West Hallandale Beach Blvd.
Hallandale, Florida 33009
(954) 456-4420

email: life@catchlife.org